From
MW01632175

THE STRANGE CASE OF DR. JEKYLL & MR. HYDE

ROBERT LOUIS STEVENSON

THE STRANGE CASE OF DR. JEKYLL & MR. HYDE

With a Full-Length SPARKNOTES Reader's Companion

SpellBinders™

This SpellBinders edition was especially created in 2004 by arrangement with Spark Publishing, a division of SparkNotes LLC.

Writers: Ross Douthat and Benjamin Lytal

The Strange Case of Dr. Jekyll & Mr. Hyde was first published in 1886

SpellBinders are published by Bookspan, 401 Franklin Avenue, Garden City, New York 11530

ISBN: 1-58288-138-3

Book design by Christos Peterson

Printed in the United States of America

CONTENTS

To

Katharine de Mattos

It's ill to loose the bands that God decreed to bind;
Still will we be the children of the heather and the wind.
Far away from home, O it's still for you and me
That the broom is blowing bonnie in the north countrie.

THE STRANGE CASE OF DR. JEKYLL & MR. HYDE

1

STORY OF THE DOOR

MR. UTTERSON THE lawyer was a man of a rugged countenance that was never lighted by a smile; cold, scanty, and embarrassed in discourse; backward in sentiment; lean, long, dusty, dreary, and yet somehow lovable. At friendly meetings, and when the wine was to his taste, something eminently human beaconed from his eye; something indeed which never found its way into his talk, but which spoke not only in these silent symbols of the after-dinner face, but more often and loudly in the acts of his life. He was austere with himself; drank gin when he was alone, to mortify a taste for vintages; and though he enjoyed the theater, had not crossed the doors of one for twenty years. But he had an approved tolerance for others; sometimes wondering, almost with envy, at the high pressure of spirits involved in their misdeeds; and in any extremity inclined to help rather than to reprove. "I incline to Cain's heresy," he used to say quaintly: "I let my brother go to the devil in his own way." In this character, it was frequently his fortune to be the last reputable acquaintance and the last good influence in the lives of down-going men. And to such as these, so long as they came about his chambers, he never marked a shade of change in his demeanor.

No doubt the feat was easy to Mr. Utterson; for he was undemonstrative at the best, and even his friendship seemed to be founded in a similar catholicity of good nature. It is the mark of a modest man to accept his friendly circle ready-made from the hands of opportunity; and that was the lawyer's way. His friends were those of his own blood or those whom he had known the longest; his affections, like ivy, were the growth of time, they implied no aptness in the object. Hence, no doubt the bond that united him to Mr. Richard Enfield, his distant kinsman, the well-known man about town. It was a nut to crack for many, what these two could see in each other, or what subject they could find in common. It was reported by those who encountered them in their Sunday walks that they said nothing, looked singularly dull, and would hail with obvious relief the appearance of a friend. For all that, the two men put the greatest store by these excursions, counted them the chief jewel of each week, and not only set aside occasions of pleasure, but even resisted the calls of business, that they might enjoy them uninterrupted.

It chanced on one of these rambles that their way led them down a bystreet in a busy quarter of London. The street was small and what is called quiet, but it drove a thriving trade on the weekdays. The inhabitants were all doing well, it seemed, and all emulously hoping to do better still, and laying out the surplus of their grains in coquetry; so that the shop fronts stood along that thoroughfare with an air of invitation, like rows of smiling saleswomen. Even on Sunday, when it veiled its more florid charms and lay comparatively empty of passage, the street shone out in contrast to its dingy neighbourhood, like a fire in a forest; and with its freshly painted shutters, well-polished brasses, and general cleanliness and gaiety of note, instantly caught and pleased the eye of the passenger.

Two doors from one corner, on the left hand going east, the line was broken by the entry of a court; and just at that point a certain sinister block of building thrust forward its gable on the street. It was two stories high; showed no window, nothing but a door on the lower story and a blind forehead of discoloured wall on the upper; and bore in every feature, the marks of prolonged and sordid negligence. The door, which was equipped with neither bell nor knocker, was blistered and distained. Tramps slouched into the recess and struck matches on the panels; children kept shop upon the steps; the schoolboy had tried his knife on the moldings; and for close on a generation, no one had appeared to drive away these random visitors or to repair their ravages.

Mr. Enfield and the lawyer were on the other side of the bystreet; but when they came abreast of the entry, the former lifted up his cane and pointed.

"Did you ever remark that door?" he asked; and when his companion had replied in the affirmative, "It is connected in my mind," added he, "with a very odd story."

"Indeed?" said Mr. Utterson, with a slight change of voice, "and what was that?"

"Well, it was this way," returned Mr. Enfield: "I was coming home from some place at the end of the world, about three o'clock of a black winter morning, and my way lay through a part of town where there was literally nothing to be seen but lamps. Street after street and all the folks asleep—street after street, all lighted up as if for a procession and all as empty as a church—till at last I got into that state of mind when a man listens and listens and begins to long for the sight of a policeman. All at once, I saw two figures: one a little man who was stumping along eastward at a good walk, and the other a girl of maybe eight or ten who was running as hard as she was able down a cross street. Well, sir, the two ran into one another naturally enough at the corner; and then came the horrible part of the thing; for the man trampled calmly over the child's body and left her screaming on the ground. It sounds nothing to hear, but it was hellish to see. It wasn't like a man; it was like some damned Juggernaut. I gave a view halloa, took to my heels, collared my gentleman, and brought him back to where there was already quite a group about the screaming child. He was perfectly cool and made no resistance, but gave me one look, so ugly that it brought out the sweat on me like running. The people who had turned out were the girl's own family; and pretty soon, the doctor, for whom she had been sent, put in his appearance. Well, the child was not much the worse, more frightened, according to the Sawbones; and there you might have supposed would be an end to it. But there was one curious circumstance. I had taken a loathing to my gentleman at first sight. So had the child's family, which was only natural. But the doctor's case was what struck me. He was the usual cut and dry apothecary, of no particular age and colour, with a strong Edinburgh accent and about as emotional as a bagpipe. Well, sir, he was like the rest of us; every time he looked at my prisoner, I saw that Sawbones turn sick and white with desire to kill him. I knew what was in his mind, just as he knew what was in mine; and killing being out of the question, we did the next best. We told the man we could and would make such a scandal out of this as should make his name stink from one end of London to the other. If he had any friends or any credit, we undertook that he should lose them. And all the time, as we were pitching it in red hot, we were keeping the women off him as best we could for they were as wild as harpies. I never saw a circle of such hateful faces; and there was the man in the middle, with a kind of black sneering coolness—frightened too, I could see that—but carrying it off, sir, really like Satan. 'If you choose to make capital out of this accident,' said he, 'I am naturally helpless. No gentleman but wishes to avoid a scene,' says he. 'Name your figure.' Well, we screwed him up to a hundred pounds for the child's family; he would have clearly liked to stick out; but there was something about the lot of us that meant mischief, and at last he struck. The next thing was to get the money; and where do you think he carried us but to that place with the door?—whipped out a key, went in, and presently came back with the matter of ten pounds in gold and a cheque for the balance on Coutts's, drawn payable to bearer and signed with a name that I can't mention, though it's one of the points of my story, but it was a name at least very well known and often printed. The figure was stiff; but the signature was good for more than that if it was only genuine. I took the liberty of pointing out to my gentleman that the whole business looked apocryphal, and that a man does not, in real life, walk into a cellar door at four in the morning and come out with another man's cheque for close upon a hundred pounds. But he was quite easy and sneering. 'Set your mind at rest,' says he, 'I will stay with you till the banks open and cash the cheque myself.' So we all set off, the doctor, and the child's father, and our friend and myself, and passed the rest of the night in my chambers; and next day, when we had breakfasted, went in a body to the bank. I gave in the cheque myself, and said I had every reason to believe it was a forgery. Not a bit of it. The cheque was genuine."

"Tut-tut," said Mr. Utterson.

"I see you feel as I do," said Mr. Enfield. "Yes, it's a bad story. For my man was a fellow that nobody could have to do with, a really damnable man; and the person that drew the cheque is the very pink of the proprieties, celebrated too, and (what makes it worse) one of your fellows who do what they call good. Blackmail I suppose; an honest man paying through the nose for some of the capers of his youth. Blackmail House is what I call the place with the door, in consequence. Though even that, you know, is far from explaining all," he added, and with the words fell into a vein of musing.

From this he was recalled by Mr. Utterson asking rather suddenly: "And you don't know if the drawer of the cheque lives there?"

"A likely place, isn't it?" returned Mr. Enfield. "But I happen to have noticed his address; he lives in some square or other."

"And you never asked about the—place with the door?" said Mr. Utterson.

"No, sir: I had a delicacy," was the reply. "I feel very strongly about putting questions; it partakes too much of the style of the day of judgment. You start a question, and it's like starting a stone. You sit quietly on the top of a hill; and away the stone goes, starting others; and presently some bland old bird (the last you would have thought of) is knocked on the head in his own back garden and the family have to change their name. No sir, I make it a rule of mine: the more it looks like Queer Street, the less I ask."

"A very good rule, too," said the lawyer.

"But I have studied the place for myself," continued Mr. Enfield. "It seems scarcely a house. There is no other door, and nobody goes in or out of that one but, once in a great while, the gentleman of my adventure. There are three windows looking on the court on the first floor; none below; the windows are always shut but they're clean. And then there is a chimney which is generally smoking; so somebody must live there. And yet it's not so sure; for the buildings are so packed together about the court, that it's hard to say where one ends and another begins."

The pair walked on again for a while in silence; and then, "Enfield," said Mr. Utterson, "that's a good rule of yours."

"Yes, I think it is," returned Enfield.

"But for all that," continued the lawyer, "there's one point I want to ask: I want to ask the name of that man who walked over the child."

"Well," said Mr. Enfield, "I can't see what harm it would do. It was a man of the name of Hyde."

"Hm," said Mr. Utterson. "What sort of a man is he to see?"

"He is not easy to describe. There is something wrong with his appearance; something displeasing, something downright detestable. I never saw a man I so disliked, and yet I scarce know why. He must be deformed somewhere; he gives a strong feeling of deformity, although I couldn't specify the point. He's an extraordinary looking man, and yet I really can name nothing out of the way. No, sir; I can make no hand of it; I can't describe him. And it's not want of memory; for I declare I can see him this moment."

Mr. Utterson again walked some way in silence and obviously under a weight of consideration. "You are sure he used a key?" he inquired at last.

"My dear sir . . ." began Enfield, surprised out of himself.

"Yes, I know," said Utterson. "I know it must seem strange. The fact is, if I do not ask you the name of the other party, it is because I know it already. You see, Richard, your tale has gone home. If you have been inexact in any point you had better correct it."

"I think you might have warned me," returned the other with a touch of sullenness. "But I have been pedantically exact, as you call it. The fellow had a key; and what's more, he has it still. I saw him use it not a week ago."

Mr. Utterson sighed deeply but said never a word; and the young man presently resumed. "Here is another lesson to say nothing," said he. "I am ashamed of my long tongue. Let us make a bargain never to refer to this again."

"With all my heart," said the lawyer. "I shake hands on that, Richard."

2

SEARCH FOR MR. HYDE

THAT EVENING MR. Utterson came home to his bachelor house in sombre spirits and sat down to dinner without relish. It was his custom of a Sunday, when this meal was over, to sit close by the fire, a volume of some dry divinity on his reading desk, until the clock of the neighbouring church rang out the hour of twelve, when he would go soberly and gratefully to bed. On this night, however, as soon as the cloth was taken away, he took up a candle and went into his business room. There he opened his safe, took from the most private part of it a document endorsed on the envelope as Dr. Jekyll's Will and sat down with a clouded brow to study its contents. The will was holograph, for Mr. Utterson, though he took charge of it now that it was made, had refused to lend the least assistance in the making of it; it provided not only that, in case of the decease of Henry Jekyll, M.D., D.C.L., L.L.D., F.R.S., etc., all his possessions were to pass into the hands of his "friend and benefactor Edward Hyde," but that in case of Dr. Jekyll's "disappearance or unexplained absence for any period exceeding three calendar months," the said Edward Hyde should step into the said Henry Jekyll's shoes without further delay and free from any burthen or obligation beyond the payment of a few small sums to the members of the doctor's household. This document had long been the lawyer's eyesore. It offended him both as a lawyer and as a lover of the sane and customary sides of life, to whom the fanciful was the immodest. And hitherto it was his ignorance of Mr. Hyde that had swelled his indignation; now, by a sudden turn, it was his knowledge. It was already bad enough when the name was but a name of which he could learn no more. It was worse when it began to be clothed upon with detestable attributes; and out of the shifting, insubstantial mists that had so long baffled his eye, there leaped up the sudden, definite presentment of a fiend.

"I thought it was madness," he said, as he replaced the obnoxious paper in the safe, "and now I begin to fear it is disgrace."

With that he blew out his candle, put on a greatcoat, and set forth in the direction of Cavendish Square, that citadel of medicine, where his friend, the great Dr. Lanyon, had his house and received his crowding patients. "If anyone knows, it will be Lanyon," he had thought.

The solemn butler knew and welcomed him; he was subjected to no stage of delay, but ushered direct from the door to the dining room where Dr. Lanyon sat alone over his wine. This was a hearty, healthy, dapper, red-faced gentleman, with a shock of hair prematurely white, and a boisterous and decided manner. At sight of Mr. Utterson, he sprang up from his chair and welcomed him with both hands. The geniality, as was the way of the man, was somewhat theatrical to the eye; but it reposed on genuine feeling. For these two were old friends, old mates both at school and college, both thorough respecters of themselves and of each other, and what does not always follow, men who thoroughly enjoyed each other's company.

After a little rambling talk, the lawyer led up to the subject which so disagreeably preoccupied his mind.

"I suppose, Lanyon," said he, "you and I must be the two oldest friends that Henry Jekyll has?"

"I wish the friends were younger," chuckled Dr. Lanyon. "But I suppose we are. And what of that? I see little of him now."

"Indeed?" said Utterson. "I thought you had a bond of common interest."

"We had," was the reply. "But it is more than ten years since Henry Jekyll became too fanciful for me. He began to go wrong, wrong in mind; and though of course I continue to take an interest in him for old sake's sake, as they say, I see and I have seen devilish little of the man. Such unscientific balderdash," added the doctor, flushing suddenly purple, "would have estranged Damon and Pythias."

This little spirit of temper was somewhat of a relief to Mr. Utterson. "They have only differed on some point of science," he thought; and being a man of no scientific passions (except in the matter of conveyancing), he even added: "It is nothing worse than that!" He gave his friend a few seconds to recover his composure, and then approached the question he had come to put. "Did you ever come across a protégé of his—one Hyde?" he asked.

"Hyde?" repeated Lanyon. "No. Never heard of him. Since my time."

That was the amount of information that the lawyer carried back with him to the great, dark bed on which he tossed to and fro, until the small hours of the morning began to grow large. It was a night of little ease to his toiling mind, toiling in mere darkness and besieged by questions.

Six o'clock struck on the bells of the church that was so conveniently near to Mr. Utterson's dwelling, and still he was digging at the problem. Hitherto it had touched him on the intellectual side alone; but now his imagination also was engaged, or rather enslaved; and as he lay and tossed in the gross darkness of the night and the curtained room, Mr. Enfield's tale went by before his mind in a scroll of lighted pictures. He would be aware of the great field of lamps of a nocturnal city; then of the figure of a man walking swiftly; then of a child running from the doctor's; and then these met, and that human Juggernaut trod the child down and passed on regardless of her screams. Or else he would see a room in a rich house, where his friend lay asleep, dreaming and smiling at his dreams; and then the door of that room would be opened, the curtains of the bed plucked apart, the sleeper recalled, and lo! there would stand by his side a figure to whom power was given, and even at that dead hour, he must rise and do its bidding. The figure in these two phases haunted the lawyer all night; and if at any time he dozed over, it was but to see it glide more stealthily through sleeping houses, or move the more swiftly and still the more swiftly, even to dizziness, through wider labyrinths of lamplighted city, and at every street corner crush a child and leave her screaming. And still the figure had no face by which he might know it; even in his dreams, it had no face, or one that baffled him and melted before his eyes; and thus it was that there sprang up and grew apace in the lawyer's mind a singularly strong, almost an inordinate, curiosity to behold the features of the real Mr. Hyde. If he could but once set eyes on him, he thought the mystery would lighten and perhaps roll altogether away, as was the habit of mysterious things when well examined. He might see a reason for his friend's strange preference or bondage (call it which you please) and even for the startling clause of the will. At least it would be a face worth seeing: the face of a man who was without bowels of mercy: a face which had but to show itself to raise up, in the mind of the unimpressionable Enfield, a spirit of enduring hatred.

From that time forward, Mr. Utterson began to haunt the door in the bystreet of shops. In the morning before office hours, at noon when business was plenty and time scarce, at night under the face of the fogged city moon, by all lights and at all hours of solitude or concourse, the lawyer was to be found on his chosen post.

"If he be Mr. Hyde," he had thought, "I shall be Mr. Seek."

And at last his patience was rewarded. It was a fine dry night; frost in the air; the streets as clean as a ballroom floor; the lamps, unshaken by any wind, drawing a regular pattern of light and shadow. By ten o'clock, when the shops were closed, the bystreet was very solitary and, in spite of the low growl of London from all round, very silent. Small sounds carried far; domestic sounds out of the houses were clearly audible on either side of the roadway; and the rumour of the approach of any passenger preceded him by a long time. Mr. Utterson had been some minutes at his post, when he was aware of an odd light footstep drawing near. In the course of his nightly patrols, he had long grown accustomed to the quaint effect with which the footfalls of a single person, while he is still a great way off, suddenly spring out distinct from the vast hum and clatter of the city. Yet his attention had never before been so sharply and decisively arrested; and it was with a strong, superstitious prevision of success that he withdrew into the entry of the court.

The steps drew swiftly nearer, and swelled out suddenly louder as they turned the end of the street. The lawyer, looking forth from the entry, could soon see what manner of man he had to deal with. He was small and very plainly dressed and the look of him, even at that distance, went somehow strongly against the watcher's inclination. But he made straight for the door, crossing the roadway to save time; and as he came, he drew a key from his pocket like one approaching home.

Mr. Utterson stepped out and touched him on the shoulder as he passed. "Mr. Hyde, I think?"

Mr. Hyde shrank back with a hissing intake of the breath. But his fear was only momentary; and though he did not look the lawyer in the face, he answered coolly enough: "That is my name. What do you want?"

"I see you are going in," returned the lawyer. "I am an old friend of Dr. Jekyll's—Mr. Utterson of Gaunt Street—you must have heard of my name; and meeting you so conveniently, I thought you might admit me."

"You will not find Dr. Jekyll; he is from home," replied Mr. Hyde, blowing in the key. And then suddenly, but still without looking up, "How did you know me?" he asked.

"On your side," said Mr. Utterson, "will you do me a favour?"

"With pleasure," replied the other. "What shall it be?"

"Will you let me see your face?" asked the lawyer.

Mr. Hyde appeared to hesitate, and then, as if upon some sudden reflection, fronted about with an air of defiance; and the pair stared at each other pretty fixedly for a few seconds. "Now I shall know you again," said Mr. Utterson. "It may be useful."

"Yes," returned Mr. Hyde, "it is as well we have met; and apropos, you should have my address." And he gave a number of a street in Soho.

"Good God!" thought Mr. Utterson, "can he, too, have been thinking of the will?" But he kept his feelings to himself and only grunted in acknowledgment of the address.

"And now," said the other, "how did you know me?"

"By description," was the reply.

"Whose description?"

"We have common friends," said Mr. Utterson.

"Common friends," echoed Mr. Hyde, a little hoarsely. "Who are they?"

"Jekyll, for instance," said the lawyer.

"He never told you," cried Mr. Hyde, with a flush of anger. "I did not think you would have lied."

"Come," said Mr. Utterson, "that is not fitting language."

The other snarled aloud into a savage laugh; and the next moment, with extraordinary quickness, he had unlocked the door and disappeared into the house.

The lawyer stood awhile when Mr. Hyde had left him, the picture of disquietude. Then he began slowly to mount the street, pausing every step or two and putting his hand to his brow like a man in mental perplexity. The problem he was thus debating as he walked was one of a class that is rarely solved. Mr. Hyde was pale and dwarfish, he gave an impression of deformity without any nameable malformation, he had a displeasing smile, he had borne himself to the lawyer with a sort of murderous mixture of timidity and boldness, and he spoke with a husky, whispering, and somewhat broken voice; all these were points against him, but not all of these together could explain the hitherto unknown disgust, loathing, and fear with which Mr. Utterson regarded him. "There must be something else," said the perplexed gentleman. "There *is* something more, if

I could find a name for it. God bless me, the man seems hardly human! Something troglodytic, shall we say? Or can it be the old story of Dr. Fell? Or is it the mere radiance of a foul soul that thus transpires through, and transfigures, its clay continent? The last, I think; for, O my poor old Harry Jekyll, if ever I read Satan's signature upon a face, it is on that of your new friend."

Round the corner from the bystreet, there was a square of ancient, handsome houses, now for the most part decayed from their high estate and let in flats and chambers to all sorts and conditions of men; map-engravers, architects, shady lawyers, and the agents of obscure enterprises. One house, however, second from the corner, was still occupied entire; and at the door of this, which wore a great air of wealth and comfort, though it was now plunged in darkness except for the fanlight, Mr. Utterson stopped and knocked. A well-dressed, elderly servant opened the door.

"Is Dr. Jekyll at home, Poole?" asked the lawyer.

"I will see, Mr. Utterson," said Poole, admitting the visitor, as he spoke, into a large, low-roofed, comfortable hall paved with flags, warmed (after the fashion of a country house) by a bright, open fire, and furnished with costly cabinets of oak. "Will you wait here by the fire, sir? Or shall I give you a light in the dining room?"

"Here, thank you," said the lawyer, and he drew near and leaned on the tall fender. This hall, in which he was now left alone, was a pet fancy of his friend the doctor's; and Utterson himself was wont to speak of it as the pleasantest room in London. But tonight there was a shudder in his blood; the face of Hyde sat heavy on his memory; he felt (what was rare with him) a nausea and distaste of life; and in the gloom of his spirits, he seemed to read a menace in the flickering of the firelight on the polished cabinets and the uneasy starting of the shadow on the roof. He was ashamed of his relief, when Poole presently returned to announce that Dr. Jekyll was gone out.

"I saw Mr. Hyde go in by the old dissecting room, Poole," he said. "Is that right, when Dr. Jekyll is from home?"

"Quite right, Mr. Utterson, sir," replied the servant. "Mr. Hyde has a key."

"Your master seems to repose a great deal of trust in that young man, Poole," resumed the other musingly.

"Yes, sir, he does indeed," said Poole. "We have all orders to obey him."

"I do not think I ever met Mr. Hyde?" asked Utterson.

"O, dear no, sir. He never *dines* here," replied the butler. "Indeed we see very little of him on this side of the house; he mostly comes and goes by the laboratory."

"Well, good-night, Poole."

"Good-night, Mr. Utterson."

And the lawyer set out homeward with a very heavy heart. "Poor Harry Jekyll," he thought, "my mind misgives me he is in deep waters! He was wild when he was young; a long while ago to be sure; but in the law of God, there is no statute of limitations. Ay, it must be that; the ghost of some old sin, the cancer of some concealed disgrace: punishment coming, *pede claudo*, years after memory has forgotten and self-love condoned the fault." And the lawyer, scared by the thought, brooded awhile on his own past, groping in all the corners of memory, least by chance some Jack-in-the-Box of an old iniquity should leap to light there. His past was fairly blameless; few men could read the rolls of their life with less apprehension; yet he was humbled to the dust by the many ill things he had done, and raised up again into a sober and fearful gratitude by the many he had come so near to doing yet avoided. And then by a return on his former subject, he conceived a spark of hope. "This Master Hyde, if he were studied," thought he, "must have secrets of his own; black secrets, by the look of him; secrets compared to which poor Jekyll's worst would be like sunshine. Things cannot continue as they are. It turns me cold to think of this creature stealing like a thief to Harry's bedside; poor Harry, what a wakening! And the danger of it; for if this Hyde suspects the existence of the will, he may grow impatient to inherit. Ay, I must put my shoulders to the wheel—if Jekyll will but let me," he added, "if Jekyll will only let me." For once more he saw before his mind's eye, as clear as transparency, the strange clauses of the will.

3

DR. JEKYLL WAS QUITE AT EASE

A FORTNIGHT LATER, by excellent good fortune, the doctor gave one of his pleasant dinners to some five or six old cronies, all intelligent, reputable men and all judges of good wine; and Mr. Utterson so contrived that he remained behind after the others had departed. This was no new arrangement, but a thing that had befallen many scores of times. Where Utterson was liked, he was liked well. Hosts loved to detain the dry lawyer, when the light-hearted and loose-tongued had already their foot on the threshold; they liked to sit a while in his unobtrusive company, practising for solitude, sobering their minds in the man's rich silence after the expense and strain of gaiety. To this rule, Dr. Jekyll was no exception; and as he now sat on the opposite side of the fire—a large, well-made, smooth-faced man of fifty, with something of a stylish cast perhaps, but every mark of capacity and kindness—you could see by his looks that he cherished for Mr. Utterson a sincere and warm affection.

"I have been wanting to speak to you, Jekyll," began the latter. "You know that will of yours?"

A close observer might have gathered that the topic was distasteful; but the doctor carried it off gaily. "My poor Utterson," said he, "you are unfortunate in such a client. I never saw a man so distressed as you were by my will; unless it were that hide-bound pedant, Lanyon, at what he called my scientific heresies. O, I know he's a good fellow—you needn't frown—an excellent fellow, and I always mean to see more of him; but a hide-bound pedant for all that; an ignorant, blatant pedant. I was never more disappointed in any man than Lanyon."

"You know I never approved of it," pursued Utterson, ruthlessly disregarding the fresh topic.

"My will? Yes, certainly, I know that," said the doctor, a trifle sharply. "You have told me so."

"Well, I tell you so again," continued the lawyer. "I have been learning something of young Hyde."

The large handsome face of Dr. Jekyll grew pale to the very lips, and there came a blackness about his eyes. "I do not care to hear more," said he. "This is a matter I thought we had agreed to drop."

"What I heard was abominable," said Utterson.

"It can make no change. You do not understand my position," returned the doctor, with a certain incoherency of manner. "I am painfully situated, Utterson; my position is a very strange—a very strange one. It is one of those affairs that cannot be mended by talking."

"Jekyll," said Utterson, "you know me: I am a man to be trusted. Make a clean breast of this in confidence; and I make no doubt I can get you out of it."

"My good Utterson," said the doctor, "this is very good of you, this is downright good of you, and I cannot find words to thank you in. I believe you fully; I would trust you before any man alive, ay, before myself, if I could make the choice; but indeed it isn't what you fancy; it is not as bad as that; and just to put your good heart at rest, I will tell you one thing: the moment I choose, I can be rid of Mr. Hyde. I give you my hand upon that; and I thank you again and again; and I will just add one little word, Utterson, that I'm sure you'll take in good part: this is a private matter, and I beg of you to let it sleep."

Utterson reflected a little, looking in the fire.

"I have no doubt you are perfectly right," he said at last, getting to his feet.

"Well, but since we have touched upon this business, and for the last time I hope," continued the doctor, "there is one point I should like you to understand. I have really a very great interest in poor Hyde. I know you have seen him; he told me so; and I fear he was rude. But I do sincerely take a great, a very great interest in that young man; and if I am taken away, Utterson, I wish you to promise me that you will bear with him and get his rights for him. I think you would, if you knew all; and it would be a weight off my mind if you would promise."

"I can't pretend that I shall ever like him," said the lawyer.

"I don't ask that," pleaded Jekyll, laying his hand upon the other's arm. "I only ask for justice; I only ask you to help him for my sake, when I am no longer here."

Utterson heaved an irrepressible sigh. "Well," said he, "I promise."

4

THE CAREW MURDER CASE

NEARLY A YEAR later, in the month of October, 18—, London was startled by a crime of singular ferocity and rendered all the more notable by the high position of the victim. The details were few and startling. A maidservant living alone in a house not far from the river, had gone upstairs to bed about eleven. Although a fog rolled over the city in the small hours, the early part of the night was cloudless, and the lane, which the maid's window overlooked, was brilliantly lit by the full moon. It seems she was romantically given, for she sat down upon her box, which stood immediately under the window, and fell into a dream of musing. Never (she used to say, with streaming tears, when she narrated that experience), never had she felt more at peace with all men or thought more kindly of the world. And as she so sat she became aware of an aged beautiful gentleman with white hair, drawing near along the lane; and advancing to meet him, another and very small gentleman, to whom at first she paid less attention. When they had come within speech (which was just under the maid's eyes) the older man bowed and accosted the other with a very pretty manner of politeness. It did not seem as if the subject of his address were of great importance; indeed, from his pointing, it sometimes appeared as if he were only inquiring his way; but the moon shone on his face as he spoke, and the girl was pleased to watch it, it seemed to breathe such an innocent and old-world kindness of disposition, yet with something high too, as of a well-founded self-content. Presently her eye wandered to the other, and she was surprised to recognise in him a certain Mr. Hyde, who had once visited her master and for whom she had conceived a dislike. He had in his hand a heavy cane, with which he was trifling; but he answered never a word, and seemed to listen with an ill-contained impatience. And then all of a sudden he broke out in a great flame of anger, stamping with his foot, brandishing the cane, and carrying on (as the maid described it) like a madman. The old gentleman took a step back, with the air of one very much surprised and a trifle hurt; and at that Mr. Hyde broke out of all bounds and clubbed him to the earth. And next moment, with ape-like fury, he was trampling his victim underfoot and hailing down a storm of blows, under which the bones were audibly shattered and the body jumped upon the roadway. At the horror of these sights and sounds, the maid fainted.

It was two o'clock when she came to herself and called for the police. The murderer was gone long ago; but there lay his victim in the middle of the lane, incredibly mangled. The stick with which the deed had been done, although it was of some rare and very tough and heavy wood, had broken in the middle under the stress of this insensate cruelty; and one splintered half had rolled in the neighbouring gutter—the other, without doubt, had been carried away by the murderer. A purse and gold watch were found upon the victim: but no cards or papers, except a sealed and stamped envelope, which he had been probably carrying to the post, and which bore the name and address of Mr. Utterson.

This was brought to the lawyer the next morning, before

he was out of bed; and he had no sooner seen it and been told the circumstances, than he shot out a solemn lip. "I shall say nothing till I have seen the body," said he; "this may be very serious. Have the kindness to wait while I dress." And with the same grave countenance he hurried through his breakfast and drove to the police station, whither the body had been carried. As soon as he came into the cell, he nodded.

"Yes," said he, "I recognise him. I am sorry to say that this is Sir Danvers Carew."

"Good God, sir," exclaimed the officer, "is it possible?" And the next moment his eye lighted up with professional ambition. "This will make a deal of noise," he said. "And perhaps you can help us to the man." And he briefly narrated what the maid had seen, and showed the broken stick.

Mr. Utterson had already quailed at the name of Hyde; but when the stick was laid before him, he could doubt no longer; broken and battered as it was, he recognized it for one that he had himself presented many years before to Henry Jekyll.

"Is this Mr. Hyde a person of small stature?" he inquired.

"Particularly small and particularly wicked-looking, is what the maid calls him," said the officer.

Mr. Utterson reflected; and then, raising his head, "If you will come with me in my cab," he said, "I think I can take you to his house."

It was by this time about nine in the morning, and the first fog of the season. A great chocolate-coloured pall lowered over heaven, but the wind was continually charging and routing these embattled vapours; so that as the cab crawled from street to street, Mr. Utterson beheld a marvelous number of degrees and hues of twilight; for here it would be dark like the back-end of evening; and there would be a glow of a rich, lurid brown, like the light of some strange conflagration; and here, for a moment, the fog would be quite broken up, and a haggard shaft of daylight would glance in between the swirling wreaths. The dismal quarter of Soho seen under these changing glimpses, with its muddy ways, and slatternly passengers, and its lamps, which had never been extinguished or had been kindled afresh to combat this mournful reinvasion of darkness, seemed, in the lawyer's eyes, like a district of some city in a nightmare. The thoughts of his mind, besides, were of the gloomiest dye; and when he glanced at the companion of his drive, he was conscious of some touch of that terror of the law and the law's officers, which may at times assail the most honest.

As the cab drew up before the address indicated, the fog lifted a little and showed him a dingy street, a gin palace, a low French eating house, a shop for the retail of penny numbers and twopenny salads, many ragged children huddled in the doorways, and many women of many different nationalities passing out, key in hand, to have a morning glass; and the next moment the fog settled down again upon that part, as brown as umber, and cut him off from his blackguardly surroundings. This was the home of Henry Jekyll's favourite; of a man who was heir to a quarter of a million sterling.

An ivory-faced and silvery-haired old woman opened the door. She had an evil face, smoothed by hypocrisy: but her manners were excellent. Yes, she said, this was Mr. Hyde's, but he was not at home; he had been in that night very late, but he had gone away again in less than an hour; there was nothing strange in that; his habits were very irregular, and he was often absent; for instance, it was nearly two months since she had seen him till yesterday.

"Very well, then, we wish to see his rooms," said the lawyer; and when the woman began to declare it was impossible, "I had better tell you who this person is," he added. "This is Inspector Newcomen of Scotland Yard."

A flash of odious joy appeared upon the woman's face. "Ah!" said she, "he is in trouble! What has he done?"

Mr. Utterson and the inspector exchanged glances. "He don't seem a very popular character," observed the latter. "And now, my good woman, just let me and this gentleman have a look about us."

In the whole extent of the house, which but for the old woman remained otherwise empty, Mr. Hyde had only used a couple of rooms; but these were furnished with luxury and good taste. A closet was filled with wine; the plate was of silver, the napery elegant; a good picture hung upon the walls, a gift (as Utterson supposed) from Henry Jekyll, who was much of a connoisseur; and the carpets were of many plies and agreeable in colour. At this moment, however, the rooms bore every mark of having been recently and hurriedly ransacked; clothes lay about the floor, with their pockets inside out; lock-fast drawers stood open; and on the hearth there lay a pile of grey ashes, as though many papers had been burned. From these embers the inspector disinterred the butt end of a green cheque book, which had resisted the action of the fire; the other half of the stick was found behind the door; and as this clinched his suspicions, the officer declared himself delighted. A visit to the bank, where several thousand pounds were found to be lying to the murderer's credit, completed his gratification.

"You may depend upon it, sir," he told Mr. Utterson: "I have him in my hand. He must have lost his head, or he never would have left the stick or, above all, burned the cheque book. Why, money's life to the man. We have nothing to do but wait for him at the bank, and get out the handbills."

This last, however, was not so easy of accomplishment; for Mr. Hyde had numbered few familiars—even the master of the servant maid had only seen him twice; his family could nowhere be traced; he had never been photographed; and the few who could describe him differed widely, as common observers will. Only on one point were they agreed; and that was the haunting sense of unexpressed deformity with which the fugitive impressed his beholders.

5

INCIDENT OF THE LETTER

IT WAS LATE in the afternoon, when Mr. Utterson found his way to Dr. Jekyll's door, where he was at once admitted by Poole, and carried down by the kitchen offices and across a yard which had once been a garden, to the building which was indifferently known as the laboratory or dissecting rooms. The doctor had bought the house from the heirs of a celebrated surgeon; and his own tastes being rather chemical than anatomical, had changed the destination of the block at the bottom of the garden. It was the first time that the lawyer had been received in that part of his friend's quarters; and he eyed the dingy, windowless structure with curiosity, and gazed round with a distasteful sense of strangeness as he crossed the theatre, once crowded with eager students and now lying gaunt and silent, the tables laden with chemical apparatus, the floor strewn with crates and littered with packing straw, and the light falling dimly through the foggy cupola. At the further end, a flight of stairs mounted to a door covered with red baize; and through this, Mr. Utterson was at last received into the doctor's cabinet. It was a large room fitted round with glass presses, furnished, among other things, with a cheval-glass and a business table, and looking out upon the court by three dusty windows barred with iron. The fire burned in the grate; a lamp was set lighted on the chimney shelf, for even in the houses the fog began to lie thickly; and there, close up to the warmth, sat Dr. Jekyll, looking deathly sick. He did not rise to meet his visitor, but held out a cold hand and bade him welcome in a changed voice.

"And now," said Mr. Utterson, as soon as Poole had left them, "you have heard the news?"

The doctor shuddered. "They were crying it in the square," he said. "I heard them in my dining room."

"One word," said the lawyer. "Carew was my client, but so are you, and I want to know what I am doing. You have not been mad enough to hide this fellow?"

"Utterson, I swear to God," cried the doctor, "I swear to God I will never set eyes on him again. I bind my honour to you that I am done with him in this world. It is all at an end. And indeed he does not want my help; you do not know him as I do; he is safe, he is quite safe; mark my words, he will never more be heard of."

The lawyer listened gloomily; he did not like his friend's feverish manner. "You seem pretty sure of him," said he; "and for your sake, I hope you may be right. If it came to a trial, your name might appear."

"I am quite sure of him," replied Jekyll. "I have grounds for certainty that I cannot share with anyone. But there is one thing on which you may advise me. I have—I have received a letter; and I am at a loss whether I should show it to the police. I should like to leave it in your hands, Utterson; you would judge wisely, I am sure; I have so great a trust in you."

"You fear, I suppose, that it might lead to his detection?" asked the lawyer.

"No," said the other. "I cannot say that I care what becomes of Hyde; I am quite done with him. I was thinking of my own character, which this hateful business has rather exposed."

Utterson ruminated awhile; he was surprised at his friend's selfishness, and yet relieved by it. "Well," said he, at last, "let me see the letter."

The letter was written in an odd, upright hand and signed "Edward Hyde": and it signified, briefly enough, that the writer's benefactor, Dr. Jekyll, whom he had long so unworthily repaid for a thousand generosities, need labour under no alarm for his safety, as he had means of escape on which he placed a sure dependence. The lawyer liked this letter well enough; it put a better colour on the intimacy than he had looked for; and he blamed himself for some of his past suspicions.

"Have you the envelope?" he asked.

"I burned it," replied Jekyll, "before I thought what I was about. But it bore no postmark. The note was handed in."

"Shall I keep this and sleep upon it?" asked Utterson.

"I wish you to judge for me entirely," was the reply. "I have lost confidence in myself."

"Well, I shall consider," returned the lawyer. "And now one word more: it was Hyde who dictated the terms in your will about that disappearance?"

The doctor seemed seized with a qualm of faintness; he shut his mouth tight and nodded.

"I knew it," said Utterson. "He meant to murder you. You had a fine escape."

"I have had what is far more to the purpose," returned the doctor solemnly: "I have had a lesson—O God, Utterson, what a lesson I have had!" And he covered his face for a moment with his hands.

On his way out, the lawyer stopped and had a word or

two with Poole. "By the bye," said he, "there was a letter handed in today: what was the messenger like?" But Poole was positive nothing had come except by post. "And only circulars by that," he added.

This news sent off the visitor with his fears renewed. Plainly the letter had come by the laboratory door; possibly, indeed, it had been written in the cabinet; and if that were so, it must be differently judged, and handled with the more caution. The newsboys, as he went, were crying themselves hoarse along the footways: "Special edition. Shocking murder of an M.P." That was the funeral oration of one friend and client; and he could not help a certain apprehension lest the good name of another should be sucked down in the eddy of the scandal. It was, at least, a ticklish decision that he had to make; and self-reliant as he was by habit, he began to cherish a longing for advice. It was not to be had directly; but perhaps, he thought, it might be fished for.

Presently after, he sat on one side of his own hearth, with Mr. Guest, his head clerk, upon the other, and midway between, at a nicely calculated distance from the fire, a bottle of a particular old wine that had long dwelt unsunned in the foundations of his house. The fog still slept on the wing above the drowned city, where the lamps glimmered like carbuncles; and through the muffle and smother of these fallen clouds, the procession of the town's life was still rolling in through the great arteries with a sound as of a mighty wind. But the room was gay with firelight. In the bottle the acids were long ago resolved; the imperial dye had softened with time, as the colour grows richer in stained windows; and the glow of hot autumn afternoons on hillside vineyards, was ready to be set free and to disperse the fogs of London. Insensibly the lawyer melted. There was no man from whom he kept fewer secrets than Mr. Guest; and he was not always sure that he kept as many as he meant. Guest had often been on business to the doctor's; he knew Poole; he could scarce have failed to hear of Mr. Hyde's familiarity about the house; he might draw conclusions: was it not as well, then, that he should see a letter which put that mystery to right? And above all since Guest, being a great student and critic of handwriting, would consider the step natural and obliging? The clerk, besides, was a man of counsel; he could scarce read so strange a document without dropping a remark; and by that remark Mr. Utterson might shape his future course.

"This is a sad business about Sir Danvers," he said.

"Yes, sir, indeed. It has elicited a great deal of public feeling," returned Guest. "The man, of course, was mad."

"I should like to hear your views on that," replied Utterson. "I have a document here in his handwriting; it is between ourselves, for I scarce know what to do about it; it is an ugly business at the best. But there it is; quite in your way: a murderer's autograph."

Guest's eyes brightened, and he sat down at once and studied it with passion. "No sir," he said: "not mad; but it is an odd hand."

"And by all accounts a very odd writer," added the lawyer.

Just then the servant entered with a note.

"Is that from Dr. Jekyll, sir?" inquired the clerk. "I thought I knew the writing. Anything private, Mr. Utterson?

"Only an invitation to dinner. Why? Do you want to see it?"

"One moment. I thank you, sir"; and the clerk laid the two sheets of paper alongside and sedulously compared their contents. "Thank you, sir," he said at last, returning both; "it's a very interesting autograph."

There was a pause, during which Mr. Utterson struggled with himself. “Why did you compare them, Guest?” he inquired suddenly.

“Well, sir,” returned the clerk, “there’s a rather singular resemblance; the two hands are in many points identical: only differently sloped.”

“Rather quaint,” said Utterson.

“It is, as you say, rather quaint,” returned Guest.

“I wouldn’t speak of this note, you know,” said the master.

“No, sir,” said the clerk. “I understand.”

But no sooner was Mr. Utterson alone that night, than he locked the note into his safe, where it reposed from that time forward. “What!” he thought. “Henry Jekyll forge for a murderer!” And his blood ran cold in his veins.

6

REMARKABLE INCIDENT OF DR. LANYON

TIME RAN ON; thousands of pounds were offered in reward, for the death of Sir Danvers was resented as a public injury; but Mr. Hyde had disappeared out of the ken of the police as though he had never existed. Much of his past was unearthed, indeed, and all disreputable: tales came out of the man's cruelty, at once so callous and violent; of his vile life, of his strange associates, of the hatred that seemed to have surrounded his career; but of his present whereabouts, not a whisper. From the time he had left the house in Soho on the morning of the murder, he was simply blotted out; and gradually, as time drew on, Mr. Utterson began to recover from the hotness of his alarm, and to grow more at quiet with himself. The death of Sir Danvers was, to his way of thinking, more than paid for by the disappearance of Mr. Hyde. Now that that evil influence had been withdrawn, a new life began for Dr. Jekyll. He came out of his seclusion, renewed relations with his friends, became once more their familiar guest and entertainer; and whilst he had always been known for charities, he was now no less distinguished for religion. He was busy, he was much in the open air, he did good; his face seemed to open and brighten, as if with an inward consciousness of service; and for more than two months, the doctor was at peace.

On the 8th of January Utterson had dined at the doctor's with a small party; Lanyon had been there; and the face of the host had looked from one to the other as in the old days when the trio were inseparable friends. On the 12th, and again on the 14th, the door was shut against the lawyer. "The doctor was confined to the house," Poole said, "and saw no one." On the 15th, he tried again, and was again refused; and having now been used for the last two months to see his friend almost daily, he found this return of solitude to weigh upon his spirits. The fifth night he had in Guest to dine with him; and the sixth he betook himself to Dr. Lanyon's.

There at least he was not denied admittance; but when he came in, he was shocked at the change which had taken place in the doctor's appearance. He had his death-warrant written legibly upon his face. The rosy man had grown pale; his flesh had fallen away; he was visibly balder and older; and yet it was not so much these tokens of a swift physical decay that arrested the lawyer's notice, as a look in the eye and quality of manner that seemed to testify to some deep-seated terror of the mind. It was unlikely that the doctor should fear death; and yet that was what Utterson was tempted to suspect. "Yes," he thought; "he is a doctor, he must know his own state and that his days are counted; and the knowledge is more than he can bear." And yet when Utterson remarked on his ill-looks, it was with an air of great firmness that Lanyon declared himself a doomed man.

"I have had a shock," he said, "and I shall never recover. It is a question of weeks. Well, life has been pleasant; I liked it; yes, sir, I used to like it. I sometimes think if we knew all, we should be more glad to get away."

"Jekyll is ill, too," observed Utterson. "Have you seen him?"

But Lanyon's face changed, and he held up a trembling hand. "I wish to see or hear no more of Dr. Jekyll," he said in a loud, unsteady voice. "I am quite done with that person; and I beg that you will spare me any allusion to one whom I regard as dead."

"Tut-tut," said Mr. Utterson; and then after a considerable pause, "Can't I do anything?" he inquired. "We are three very old friends, Lanyon; we shall not live to make others."

"Nothing can be done," returned Lanyon; "ask himself."

"He will not see me," said the lawyer.

"I am not surprised at that," was the reply. "Some day, Utterson, after I am dead, you may perhaps come to learn the right and wrong of this. I cannot tell you. And in the meantime, if you can sit and talk with me of other things, for God's sake, stay and do so; but if you cannot keep clear of this accursed topic, then in God's name, go, for I cannot bear it."

As soon as he got home, Utterson sat down and wrote to Jekyll, complaining of his exclusion from the house, and asking the cause of this unhappy break with Lanyon; and the next day brought him a long answer, often very pathetically worded, and sometimes darkly mysterious in drift. The quarrel with Lanyon was incurable. "I do not blame our old friend," Jekyll wrote, "but I share his view that we must never meet. I mean from henceforth to lead a life of extreme seclusion; you must not be surprised, nor must you doubt my friendship, if my door is often shut even to you. You must suffer me to go my own dark way. I have brought on myself a punishment and a danger that I cannot name. If I am the chief of sinners, I am the chief of sufferers also. I could not think that this earth contained a place for sufferings and terrors so unmanning; and you can do but one thing, Utterson, to lighten this destiny, and that is to respect my silence." Utterson was amazed; the dark influence of Hyde had been withdrawn, the doctor had returned to his old tasks and amities; a week ago, the prospect had smiled with every promise of a cheerful and an honoured age; and now in a moment, friendship, and peace of mind, and the whole tenor of his life were wrecked. So great and unprepared a change pointed to madness; but in view of Lanyon's manner and words, there must lie for it some deeper ground.

A week afterwards Dr. Lanyon took to his bed, and in something less than a fortnight he was dead. The night after the funeral, at which he had been sadly affected, Utterson locked the door of his business room, and sitting there by the light of a melancholy candle, drew out and set before him an envelope addressed by the hand and sealed with the seal of his dead friend. "PRIVATE: for the hands of G. J. Utterson ALONE, and in case of his predecease *to be destroyed unread*," so it was emphatically superscribed; and the lawyer dreaded to behold the contents. "I have buried one friend today," he thought: "what if this should cost me another?" And then he condemned the fear as a disloyalty, and broke the seal. Within there was another enclosure, likewise sealed, and marked upon the cover as "not to be opened till the death or disappearance of Dr. Henry Jekyll." Utterson could not trust his eyes. Yes, it was disappearance; here again, as in the mad will which he had long ago restored to its author, here again were the idea of a disappearance and the name of Henry Jekyll bracketed. But in the will that idea had sprung from the sinister suggestion of the man Hyde; it was set there with a purpose all too plain and horrible. Written by the hand of Lanyon, what should it mean? A great curiosity came on the trustee, to disregard the prohibition and dive at once to the bottom of these mysteries; but professional honour and faith to his dead friend were stringent obligations; and the packet slept in the inmost corner of his private safe.

It is one thing to mortify curiosity, another to conquer it; and it may be doubted if, from that day forth, Utterson desired the society of his surviving friend with the same eagerness. He thought of him kindly; but his thoughts were disquieted and fearful. He went to call indeed; but he was perhaps relieved to be denied admittance; perhaps, in his heart, he preferred to speak with Poole upon the doorstep and surrounded by the air and sounds of the open city, rather than to be admitted into that house of voluntary bondage, and to sit and speak with its inscrutable recluse. Poole had, indeed, no very pleasant news to communicate. The doctor, it appeared, now more than ever confined himself to the cabinet over the laboratory, where he would sometimes even sleep; he was out of spirits, he had grown very silent, he did not read; it seemed as if he had something on his mind. Utterson became so used to the unvarying character of these reports that he fell off little by little in the frequency of his visits.

7

INCIDENT AT THE WINDOW

IT CHANCED ON Sunday, when Mr. Utterson was on his usual walk with Mr. Enfield, that their way lay once again through the bystreet; and that when they came in front of the door, both stopped to gaze on it.

"Well," said Enfield, "that story's at an end at least. We shall never see more of Mr. Hyde."

"I hope not," said Utterson. "Did I ever tell you that I once saw him, and shared your feeling of repulsion?"

"It was impossible to do the one without the other," returned Enfield. "And by the way, what an ass you must have thought me, not to know that this was a back way to Dr. Jekyll's! It was partly your own fault that I found it out, even when I did."

"So you found it out, did you?" said Utterson. "But if that be so, we may step into the court and take a look at the windows. To tell you the truth, I am uneasy about poor Jekyll; and even outside, I feel as if the presence of a friend might do him good."

The court was very cool and a little damp, and full of premature twilight, although the sky, high up overhead, was still bright with sunset. The middle one of the three windows was halfway open; and sitting close beside it, taking the air with an infinite sadness of mien, like some disconsolate prisoner, Utterson saw Dr. Jekyll.

"What! Jekyll!" he cried. "I trust you are better."

"I am very low, Utterson," replied the doctor drearily, "very low. It will not last long, thank God."

"You stay too much indoors," said the lawyer. "You should be out, whipping up the circulation like Mr. Enfield and me. (This is my cousin—Mr. Enfield—Dr. Jekyll.) Come now; get your hat and take a quick turn with us."

"You are very good," sighed the other. "I should like to very much; but no, no, no, it is quite impossible; I dare not. But indeed, Utterson, I am very glad to see you; this is really a great pleasure; I would ask you and Mr. Enfield up, but the place is really not fit."

"Why, then," said the lawyer, good-naturedly, "the best thing we can do is to stay down here and speak with you from where we are."

"That is just what I was about to venture to propose," returned the doctor with a smile. But the words were hardly uttered, before the smile was struck out of his face and succeeded by an expression of such abject terror and despair, as froze the very blood of the two gentlemen below. They saw it but for a glimpse, for the window was instantly thrust down; but that glimpse had been sufficient, and they turned and left the court without a word. In silence, too, they traversed the bystreet; and it was not until they had come into a neighbouring thoroughfare, where even upon a Sunday there were still some stirrings of life, that Mr. Utterson at last turned and looked at his companion. They were both pale; and there was an answering horror in their eyes.

"God forgive us, God forgive us," said Mr. Utterson.

But Mr. Enfield only nodded his head very seriously, and walked on once more in silence.

8

THE LAST NIGHT

MR. UTTERSON WAS sitting by his fireside one evening after dinner, when he was surprised to receive a visit from Poole.

"Bless me, Poole, what brings you here?" he cried. And then taking a second look at him, "What ails you?" he added. "Is the doctor ill?"

"Mr. Utterson," said the man, "there is something wrong."

"Take a seat, and here is a glass of wine for you," said the lawyer. "Now, take your time, and tell me plainly what you want."

"You know the doctor's ways, sir," replied Poole, "and how he shuts himself up. Well, he's shut up again in the cabinet; and I don't like it, sir—I wish I may die if I like it. Mr. Utterson, sir, I'm afraid."

"Now, my good man," said the lawyer, "be explicit. What are you afraid of?"

"I've been afraid for about a week," returned Poole, doggedly disregarding the question, "and I can bear it no more."

The man's appearance amply bore out his words; his manner was altered for the worse; and except for the moment when he had first announced his terror, he had not once looked the lawyer in the face. Even now, he sat with the glass of wine untasted on his knee, and his eyes directed to a corner of the floor. "I can bear it no more," he repeated.

"Come," said the lawyer, "I see you have some good reason, Poole; I see there is something seriously amiss. Try to tell me what it is."

"I think there's been foul play," said Poole, hoarsely.

"Foul play!" cried the lawyer, a good deal frightened and rather inclined to be irritated in consequence. "What foul play! What does the man mean?"

"I daren't say, sir," was the answer; "but will you come along with me and see for yourself?"

Mr. Utterson's only answer was to rise and get his hat and greatcoat; but he observed with wonder the greatness of the relief that appeared upon the butler's face, and perhaps with no less, that the wine was still untasted when he set it down to follow.

It was a wild, cold, seasonable night of March, with a pale moon, lying on her back as though the wind had tilted her, and flying wrack of the most diaphanous and lawny texture. The wind made talking difficult, and flecked the blood into the face. It seemed to have swept the streets unusually bare of passengers, besides; for Mr. Utterson thought he had never seen that part of London so deserted. He could have wished it otherwise; never in his life had he been conscious of so sharp a wish to see and touch his fellow creatures; for struggle as he might, there was borne in upon his mind a crushing anticipation of calamity. The square, when they got there, was full of wind and dust, and the thin trees in the garden were lashing themselves along the railing. Poole, who had kept all the way a pace or two ahead, now pulled up in the middle of the pavement, and in spite of the biting weather, took off his hat and mopped his brow with a red pocket-handkerchief. But for all the hurry of his coming, these were not the dews of exertion that he wiped away, but the moisture of some strangling anguish; for his face was white and his voice, when he spoke, harsh and broken.

"Well, sir," he said, "here we are, and God grant there be nothing wrong."

"Amen, Poole," said the lawyer.

Thereupon the servant knocked in a very guarded manner; the door was opened on the chain; and a voice asked from within, "Is that you, Poole?"

"It's all right," said Poole. "Open the door."

The hall, when they entered it, was brightly lighted up; the fire was built high; and about the hearth the whole of the servants, men and women, stood huddled together like a flock of sheep. At the sight of Mr. Utterson, the housemaid broke into hysterical whimpering; and the cook, crying out "Bless God! It's Mr. Utterson," ran forward as if to take him in her arms.

"What, what? Are you all here?" said the lawyer peevishly. "Very irregular, very unseemly; your master would be far from pleased."

"They're all afraid," said Poole.

Blank silence followed, no one protesting; only the maid lifted her voice and now wept loudly.

"Hold your tongue!" Poole said to her, with a ferocity of accent that testified to his own jangled nerves; and indeed, when the girl had so suddenly raised the note of her lamentation, they had all started and turned towards the inner door with faces of dreadful expectation. "And now," continued the butler, addressing the knife-boy, "reach me a candle, and we'll get this through hands at once." And then he begged Mr. Utterson to follow him, and led the way to the back garden.

"Now, sir," said he, "you come as gently as you can. I want you to hear, and I don't want you to be heard. And see here, sir, if by any chance he was to ask you in, don't go."

Mr. Utterson's nerves, at this unlooked-for termination, gave a jerk that nearly threw him from his balance; but he recollected his courage and followed the butler into the laboratory building through the surgical theatre, with its lumber of crates and bottles, to the foot of the stair. Here Poole motioned him to stand on one side and listen; while he himself, setting down the candle and making a great and obvious call on his resolution, mounted the steps and knocked with a somewhat uncertain hand on the red baize of the cabinet door.

"Mr. Utterson, sir, asking to see you," he called; and even as he did so, once more violently signed to the lawyer to give ear.

A voice answered from within: "Tell him I cannot see anyone," it said complainingly.

"Thank you, sir," said Poole, with a note of something like triumph in his voice; and taking up his candle, he led Mr. Utterson back across the yard and into the great kitchen, where the fire was out and the beetles were leaping on the floor.

"Sir," he said, looking Mr. Utterson in the eyes, "was that my master's voice?"

"It seems much changed," replied the lawyer, very pale, but giving look for look.

"Changed? Well, yes, I think so," said the butler. "Have I been twenty years in this man's house, to be deceived about his voice? No, sir; master's made away with; he was made away with eight days ago, when we heard him cry out upon the name of God; and *who's* in there instead of him, and *why* it stays there, is a thing that cries to Heaven, Mr. Utterson!"

"This is a very strange tale, Poole; this is rather a wild tale, my man," said Mr. Utterson, biting his finger. "Suppose it were as you suppose, supposing Dr. Jekyll to have been—well, murdered, what could induce the murderer to stay? That won't hold water; it doesn't commend itself to reason."

"Well, Mr. Utterson, you are a hard man to satisfy, but I'll do it yet," said Poole. "All this last week (you must know) him, or it, whatever it is that lives in that cabinet, has been crying night and day for some sort of medicine and cannot get it to his mind. It was sometimes his way—the master's, that is—to write his orders on a sheet of paper and throw it on the stair. We've had nothing else this week back; nothing but papers, and a closed door, and the very meals left there to be smuggled in when nobody was looking. Well, sir, every day, ay, and twice and thrice in the same day, there have been orders and complaints, and I have been sent flying to all the wholesale chemists in town. Every time I brought the stuff back, there would be another paper telling me to return it, because it was not pure, and another order to a different firm. This drug is wanted bitter bad, sir, whatever for."

"Have you any of these papers?" asked Mr. Utterson.

Poole felt in his pocket and handed out a crumpled note, which the lawyer, bending nearer to the candle, carefully examined. Its contents ran thus: "Dr. Jekyll presents his compliments to Messrs. Maw. He assures them that their last sample is impure and quite useless for his present purpose. In the year 18—, Dr. J. purchased a somewhat large quantity from Messrs. M. He now begs them to search with most sedulous care, and should any of the same quality be left, forward it to him at once. Expense is no consideration.

The importance of this to Dr. J. can hardly be exaggerated." So far the letter had run composedly enough, but here with a sudden splutter of the pen, the writer's emotion had broken loose. "For God's sake," he added, "find me some of the old."

"This is a strange note," said Mr. Utterson; and then sharply, "How do you come to have it open?"

"The man at Maw's was main angry, sir, and he threw it back to me like so much dirt," returned Poole.

"This is unquestionably the doctor's hand, do you know?" resumed the lawyer.

"I thought it looked like it," said the servant rather sulkily; and then, with another voice, "But what matters hand of write?" he said. "I've seen him!"

"Seen him?" repeated Mr. Utterson. "Well?"

"That's it!" said Poole. "It was this way. I came suddenly into the theatre from the garden. It seems he had slipped out to look for this drug or whatever it is; for the cabinet door was open, and there he was at the far end of the room digging among the crates. He looked up when I came in, gave a kind of cry, and whipped upstairs into the cabinet. It was but for one minute that I saw him, but the hair stood upon my head like quills. Sir, if that was my master, why had he a mask upon his face? If it was my master, why did he cry out like a rat, and run from me? I have served him long enough. And then . . ." The man paused and passed his hand over his face.

"These are all very strange circumstances," said Mr. Utterson, "but I think I begin to see daylight. Your master, Poole, is plainly seized with one of those maladies that both torture and deform the sufferer; hence, for aught I know, the alteration of his voice; hence the mask and the avoidance of his friends; hence his eagerness to find this drug, by means of which the poor soul retains some hope of ultimate recovery—God grant that he be not deceived! There is my explanation; it is sad enough, Poole, ay, and appalling to consider; but it is plain and natural, hangs well together, and delivers us from all exorbitant alarms."

"Sir," said the butler, turning to a sort of mottled pallor, "that thing was not my master, and there's the truth. My master"—here he looked round him and began to whisper—"is a tall, fine build of a man, and this was more of a dwarf." Utterson attempted to protest. "O, sir," cried Poole, "do you think I do not know my master after twenty years? Do you think I do not know where his head comes to in the cabinet door, where I saw him every morning of my life? No, sir, that thing in the mask was never Dr. Jekyll—God knows what it was, but it was never Dr. Jekyll; and it is the belief of my heart that there was murder done."

"Poole," replied the lawyer, "if you say that, it will become my duty to make certain. Much as I desire to spare your master's feelings, much as I am puzzled by this note which seems to prove him to be still alive, I shall consider it my duty to break in that door."

"Ah, Mr. Utterson, that's talking!" cried the butler.

"And now comes the second question," resumed Utterson: "Who is going to do it?"

"Why, you and me, sir," was the undaunted reply.

"That's very well said," returned the lawyer; "and whatever comes of it, I shall make it my business to see you are no loser."

"There is an axe in the theatre," continued Poole; "and you might take the kitchen poker for yourself."

The lawyer took that rude but weighty instrument into

his hand, and balanced it. "Do you know, Poole," he said, looking up, "that you and I are about to place ourselves in a position of some peril?"

"You may say so, sir, indeed," returned the butler.

"It is well, then that we should be frank," said the other. "We both think more than we have said; let us make a clean breast. This masked figure that you saw, did you recognise it?"

"Well, sir, it went so quick, and the creature was so doubled up, that I could hardly swear to that," was the answer. "But if you mean, was it Mr. Hyde?—why, yes, I think it was! You see, it was much of the same bigness; and it had the same quick, light way with it; and then who else could have got in by the laboratory door? You have not forgot, sir, that at the time of the murder he had still the key with him? But that's not all. I don't know, Mr. Utterson, if you ever met this Mr. Hyde?"

"Yes," said the lawyer, "I once spoke with him."

"Then you must know as well as the rest of us that there was something queer about that gentleman—something that gave a man a turn—I don't know rightly how to say it, sir, beyond this: that you felt in your marrow kind of cold and thin."

"I own I felt something of what you describe," said Mr. Utterson.

"Quite so, sir," returned Poole. "Well, when that masked thing like a monkey jumped from among the chemicals and whipped into the cabinet, it went down my spine like ice. O, I know it's not evidence, Mr. Utterson; I'm book-learned enough for that; but a man has his feelings, and I give you my bible word it was Mr. Hyde!"

"Ay, ay," said the lawyer. "My fears incline to the same point. Evil, I fear, founded—evil was sure to come—of that connection. Ay truly, I believe you; I believe poor Harry is killed; and I believe his murderer (for what purpose, God alone can tell) is still lurking in his victim's room. Well, let our name be vengeance. Call Bradshaw."

The footman came at the summons, very white and nervous.

"Put yourself together, Bradshaw," said the lawyer. "This suspense, I know, is telling upon all of you; but it is now our intention to make an end of it. Poole, here, and I are going to force our way into the cabinet. If all is well, my shoulders are broad enough to bear the blame. Meanwhile, lest anything should really be amiss, or any malefactor seek to escape by the back, you and the boy must go round the corner with a pair of good sticks and take your post at the laboratory door. We give you ten minutes, to get to your stations."

As Bradshaw left, the lawyer looked at his watch. "And now, Poole, let us get to ours," he said; and taking the poker under his arm, led the way into the yard. The scud had banked over the moon, and it was now quite dark. The wind, which only broke in puffs and draughts into that deep well of building, tossed the light of the candle to and fro about their steps, until they came into the shelter of the theatre, where they sat down silently to wait. London hummed solemnly all around; but nearer at hand, the stillness was only broken by the sounds of a footfall moving to and fro along the cabinet floor.

"So it will walk all day, sir," whispered Poole; "ay, and the better part of the night. Only when a new sample comes from the chemist, there's a bit of a break. Ah, it's an ill conscience that's such an enemy to rest! Ah, sir, there's blood foully shed in every step of it! But hark again, a little closer—put your heart in your ears, Mr. Utterson, and tell me, is that the doctor's foot?"

The steps fell lightly and oddly, with a certain swing, for all they went so slowly; it was different indeed from the heavy creaking tread of Henry Jekyll. Utterson sighed. "Is there never anything else?" he asked.

Poole nodded. "Once," he said. "Once I heard it weeping!"

"Weeping? how that?" said the lawyer, conscious of a sudden chill of horror.

"Weeping like a woman or a lost soul," said the butler. "I came away with that upon my heart, that I could have wept too."

But now the ten minutes drew to an end. Poole disinterred the axe from under a stack of packing straw; the candle was set upon the nearest table to light them to the attack; and they drew near with bated breath to where that patient foot was still going up and down, up and down, in the quiet of the night. "Jekyll," cried Utterson, with a loud voice, "I demand to see you." He paused a moment, but there came no reply. "I give you fair warning, our suspicions are aroused, and I must and shall see you," he resumed; "if not by fair means, then by foul—if not of your consent, then by brute force!"

"Utterson," said the voice, "for God's sake, have mercy!"

"Ah, that's not Jekyll's voice—it's Hyde's!" cried Utterson. "Down with the door, Poole!"

Poole swung the axe over his shoulder; the blow shook the building, and the red baize door leaped against the lock and hinges. A dismal screech, as of mere animal terror, rang from the cabinet. Up went the axe again, and again the panels crashed and the frame bounded; four times the blow fell; but the wood was tough and the fittings were of excellent workmanship; and it was not until the fifth, that the lock burst and the wreck of the door fell inwards on the carpet.

The besiegers, appalled by their own riot and the stillness that had succeeded, stood back a little and peered in. There lay the cabinet before their eyes in the quiet lamplight, a good fire glowing and chattering on the hearth, the kettle singing its thin strain, a drawer or two open, papers neatly set forth on the business table, and nearer the fire, the things laid out for tea; the quietest room, you would have said, and, but for the glazed presses full of chemicals, the most commonplace that night in London.

Right in the middle there lay the body of a man sorely contorted and still twitching. They drew near on tiptoe, turned it on its back and beheld the face of Edward Hyde. He was dressed in clothes far too large for him, clothes of the doctor's bigness; the cords of his face still moved with a semblance of life, but life was quite gone: and by the crushed phial in the hand and the strong smell of kernels that hung upon the air, Utterson knew that he was looking on the body of a self-destroyer.

"We have come too late," he said sternly, "whether to save or punish. Hyde is gone to his account; and it only remains for us to find the body of your master."

The far greater proportion of the building was occupied by the theatre, which filled almost the whole ground story and was lighted from above, and by the cabinet, which formed an upper story at one end and looked upon the court. A corridor joined the theatre to the door on the bystreet; and with this the cabinet communicated separately by a second flight of stairs. There were besides a few dark closets and a spacious cellar. All these they now thoroughly examined. Each closet needed but a glance, for all were empty, and all, by the dust that fell from their doors, had stood long unopened. The cellar, indeed, was filled with crazy lumber, mostly dating from the times of the surgeon who was Jekyll's predecessor; but even as they opened the door they were advertised of the uselessness of further search, by the fall of a perfect mat of cobweb which had for years sealed up the entrance. Nowhere was there any trace of Henry Jekyll, dead or alive.

Poole stamped on the flags of the corridor. "He must be buried here," he said, hearkening to the sound.

"Or he may have fled," said Utterson, and he turned to examine the door in the bystreet. It was locked; and lying near-by on the flags, they found the key, already stained with rust.

"This does not look like use," observed the lawyer.

"Use!" echoed Poole. "Do you not see, sir, it is broken? Much as if a man had stamped on it."

"Ay," continued Utterson, "and the fractures, too, are rusty." The two men looked at each other with a scare. "This is beyond me, Poole," said the lawyer. "Let us go back to the cabinet."

They mounted the stair in silence, and still with an occasional awestruck glance at the dead body, proceeded more thoroughly to examine the contents of the cabinet. At one table, there were traces of chemical work, various measured heaps of some white salt being laid on glass saucers, as though for an experiment in which the unhappy man had been prevented.

"That is the same drug that I was always bringing him," said Poole; and even as he spoke, the kettle with a startling noise boiled over.

This brought them to the fireside, where the easy chair was drawn cosily up, and the tea things stood ready to the sitter's elbow, the very sugar in the cup. There were several books on a shelf; one lay beside the tea things open, and Utterson was amazed to find it a copy of a pious work, for which Jekyll had several times expressed a great esteem, annotated, in his own hand, with startling blasphemies.

Next, in the course of their review of the chamber, the searchers came to the cheval-glass, into whose depths they looked with an involuntary horror. But it was so turned as to show them nothing but the rosy glow playing on the roof, the fire sparkling in a hundred repetitions along the glazed front of the presses, and their own pale and fearful countenances stooping to look in.

"This glass has seen some strange things, sir," whispered Poole.

"And surely none stranger than itself," echoed the lawyer in the same tones. "For what did Jekyll"—he caught himself up at the word with a start, and then conquering the weakness—"what could Jekyll want with it?" he said.

"You may say that!" said Poole.

Next they turned to the business table. On the desk, among the neat array of papers, a large envelope was uppermost, and bore, in the doctor's hand, the name of Mr. Utterson. The lawyer unsealed it, and several enclosures fell to the floor. The first was a will, drawn in the same eccentric terms as the one which he had returned six months before, to serve as a testament in case of death and as a deed of gift in case of disappearance; but in place of the name of Edward Hyde, the lawyer, with indescribable amazement read the name of Gabriel John Utterson. He looked at Poole, and then back at the paper, and last of all at the dead malefactor stretched upon the carpet.

"My head goes round," he said. "He has been all these

days in possession; he had no cause to like me; he must have raged to see himself displaced; and he has not destroyed this document."

He caught up the next paper; it was a brief note in the doctor's hand and dated at the top. "O Poole!" the lawyer cried, "he was alive and here this day. He cannot have been disposed of in so short a space; he must be still alive, he must have fled! And then, why fled? And how? And in that case, can we venture to declare this suicide? O, we must be careful. I foresee that we may yet involve your master in some dire catastrophe."

"Why don't you read it, sir?" asked Poole.

"Because I fear," replied the lawyer solemnly. "God grant I have no cause for it!" And with that he brought the paper to his eyes and read as follows:

> My dear Utterson,—When this shall fall into your hands, I shall have disappeared, under what circumstances I have not the penetration to foresee, but my instinct and all the circumstances of my nameless situation tell me that the end is sure and must be early. Go then, and first read the narrative which Lanyon warned me he was to place in your hands; and if you care to hear more, turn to the confession of
>
> Your unworthy and unhappy friend,
> HENRY JEKYLL.

"There was a third enclosure?" asked Utterson.

"Here, sir," said Poole, and gave into his hands a considerable packet sealed in several places.

The lawyer put it in his pocket. "I would say nothing of

this paper. If your master has fled or is dead, we may at least save his credit. It is now ten; I must go home and read these documents in quiet; but I shall be back before midnight, when we shall send for the police."

They went out, locking the door of the theatre behind them; and Utterson, once more leaving the servants gathered about the fire in the hall, trudged back to his office to read the two narratives in which this mystery was now to be explained.

9

DR. LANYON'S NARRATIVE

ON THE NINTH of January, now four days ago, I received by the evening delivery a registered envelope, addressed in the hand of my colleague and old school companion, Henry Jekyll. I was a good deal surprised by this; for we were by no means in the habit of correspondence; I had seen the man, dined with him, indeed, the night before; and I could imagine nothing in our intercourse that should justify formality of registration. The contents increased my wonder; for this is how the letter ran:

10th December, 18—.

Dear Lanyon,—You are one of my oldest friends; and although we may have differed at times on scientific questions, I cannot remember, at least on my side, any break in our affection. There was never a day when, if you had said to me, "Jekyll, my life, my honour, my reason, depend upon you," I would not have sacrificed my left hand to help you. Lanyon, my life, my honour, my reason, are all at your mercy; if you fail me tonight, I am lost. You might suppose, after this preface, that I am going to ask you for something dishonourable to grant. Judge for yourself.

I want you to postpone all other engagements for tonight—ay, even if you were summoned to the bedside of an emperor; to take a cab, unless your carriage should be actually at the door; and with this letter in your hand for consultation, to drive straight to my house. Poole, my butler, has his orders; you will find him waiting your arrival with a locksmith. The door of my cabinet is then to be forced: and you are to go in alone; to open the glazed press (letter E) on the left hand, breaking the lock if it be shut; and to draw out, *with all its contents as they stand*, the fourth drawer from the top or (which is the same thing) the third from the bottom. In my extreme distress of mind, I have a morbid fear of misdirecting you; but even if I am in error, you may know the right drawer by its contents: some powders, a phial, and a paper book. This drawer I beg of you to carry back with you to Cavendish Square exactly as it stands.

That is the first part of the service: now for the second. You should be back, if you set out at once on the receipt of this, long before midnight; but I will leave you that amount of margin, not only in the fear of one of those obstacles that can neither be prevented nor foreseen, but because an hour when your servants are in bed is to be preferred for what will then remain to do. At midnight, then, I have to ask you to be alone in your consulting room, to admit with your own hand into the house a man who will present himself in my name, and to place in his hands the drawer that you will have brought with you from my cabinet. Then you will have played your part and earned my gratitude completely. Five minutes afterwards, if you insist upon an explanation, you will have understood that these arrangements are of capital importance; and that by the neglect of one of them, fantastic as they must appear, you might have charged your conscience with my death or the shipwreck of my reason.

Confident as I am that you will not trifle with this appeal, my heart sinks and my hand trembles at the bare thought of such a possibility. Think of me at this hour, in a strange place, labouring under a blackness of distress that no fancy can exaggerate, and yet well aware that, if you will but punctually serve me, my troubles will roll away like a story that is told. Serve me, my dear Lanyon and save

Your friend,
H. J.

P.S.—I had already sealed this up when a fresh terror struck upon my soul. It is possible that the post office may fail me, and this letter not come into your hands until tomorrow morning. In that case, dear Lanyon, do my errand when it shall be most convenient for you in the course of the day; and once more expect my messenger at midnight. It may then already be too late; and if that night passes without event, you will know that you have seen the last of Henry Jekyll.

Upon the reading of this letter, I made sure my colleague was insane; but till that was proved beyond the possibility of doubt, I felt bound to do as he requested. The less I understood of this farrago, the less I was in a position to judge of its importance; and an appeal so worded could not be set aside without a grave responsibility. I rose accordingly from table, got into a hansom, and drove straight to Jekyll's house. The butler was awaiting my arrival; he had received by the same post as mine a registered letter of instruction, and had sent at once for a locksmith and a carpenter. The tradesmen came while we were yet speaking; and we moved in a body to old Dr. Denman's surgical theatre, from which (as you are doubtless aware) Jekyll's private cabinet is most conveniently entered. The door was very strong, the lock excellent; the carpenter avowed he would have great trouble and have to do much damage, if force were to be used; and the locksmith was near despair. But this last was a handy fellow, and after two hour's work, the door stood open. The press marked E was unlocked; and I took out the drawer, had it filled up with straw and tied in a sheet, and returned with it to Cavendish Square.

Here I proceeded to examine its contents. The powders were neatly enough made up, but not with the nicety of the dispensing chemist; so that it was plain they were of Jekyll's private manufacture: and when I opened one of the wrappers I found what seemed to me a simple crystalline salt of a white colour. The phial, to which I next turned my attention, might have been about half full of a blood-red liquor, which was highly pungent to the sense of smell and seemed to me to contain phosphorus and some volatile ether. At the other ingredients I could make no guess. The book was an ordinary version book and contained little but a series of dates. These covered a period of many years, but I observed that the entries ceased nearly a year ago and quite abruptly. Here and there a brief remark was appended to a date, usually no more than a single word: "double" occurring perhaps six times in a total of several hundred entries; and once very early in the list and followed by several marks of exclamation, "total failure!!!" All this, though it whetted my curiosity, told me little that was definite. Here were a phial of some salt, and the record of a series of experiments that had led (like too many of Jekyll's investigations) to no end of practical usefulness. How could the presence of these articles in my house affect either the honour, the sanity, or the life of my flighty colleague? If his messenger could go to one place, why could he not go to another? And even granting some impediment, why was this gentleman to be received by me in secret? The more I reflected the more convinced I grew that I was dealing with a case of cerebral disease; and though I dismissed my servants to bed, I loaded an old revolver, that I might be found in some posture of self-defence.

Twelve o'clock had scarce rung out over London, ere the knocker sounded very gently on the door. I went myself at the summons, and found a small man crouching against the pillars of the portico.

"Are you come from Dr. Jekyll?" I asked.

He told me "yes" by a constrained gesture; and when I had bidden him enter, he did not obey me without a searching backward glance into the darkness of the square. There was a policeman not far off, advancing with his bull's-eye open; and at the sight, I thought my visitor started and made greater haste.

These particulars struck me, I confess, disagreeably; and as I followed him into the bright light of the consulting room, I kept my hand ready on my weapon. Here, at last, I had a chance of clearly seeing him. I had never set eyes on him before, so much was certain. He was small, as I have said; I was struck besides with the shocking expression of his face, with his remarkable combination of great muscular activity and great apparent debility of constitution, and—last but not least—with the odd, subjective disturbance caused by his neighbourhood. This bore some resemblance to incipient rigour, and was accompanied by a marked sinking of the pulse. At the time, I set it down to some idiosyncratic, personal distaste, and merely wondered at the acuteness of the symptoms; but I have since had reason to believe the cause to lie much deeper in the nature of man, and to turn on some nobler hinge than the principle of hatred.

This person (who had thus, from the first moment of his entrance, struck in me what I can only describe as a disgustful curiosity) was dressed in a fashion that would have made an ordinary person laughable; his clothes, that is to say, although they were of rich and sober fabric, were enormously too large for him in every measurement—the trousers hanging on his legs and rolled up to keep them from the ground, the waist of the coat below his haunches, and the collar sprawling wide upon his shoulders. Strange to relate, this ludicrous accoutrement was far from moving me to laughter. Rather, as there was something abnormal and misbegotten in the very essence of the creature that now faced me—something seizing, surprising, and revolting—this fresh disparity seemed but to fit in with and to reinforce it; so that to my interest in the man's nature and character, there was added a curiosity as to his origin, his life, his fortune and status in the world.

These observations, though they have taken so great a space to be set down in, were yet the work of a few seconds. My visitor was, indeed, on fire with sombre excitement.

"Have you got it?" he cried. "Have you got it?" And so lively was his impatience that he even laid his hand upon my arm and sought to shake me.

I put him back, conscious at his touch of a certain icy pang along my blood. "Come, sir," said I. "You forget that I have not yet the pleasure of your acquaintance. Be seated, if you please." And I showed him an example, and sat down myself in my customary seat and with as fair an imitation of my ordinary manner to a patient, as the lateness of the hour, the nature of my preoccupations, and the horror I had of my visitor, would suffer me to muster.

"I beg your pardon, Dr. Lanyon," he replied civilly enough. "What you say is very well founded; and my impatience has shown its heels to my politeness. I come here at the instance of your colleague, Dr. Henry Jekyll, on a piece of business of some moment; and I understood . . ." He paused and put his hand to his throat, and I could see, in spite of his collected manner, that he was wrestling against the approaches of the hysteria—"I understood, a drawer . . ."

But here I took pity on my visitor's suspense, and some perhaps on my own growing curiosity.

"There it is, sir," said I, pointing to the drawer, where it lay on the floor behind a table and still covered with the sheet.

He sprang to it, and then paused, and laid his hand upon his heart: I could hear his teeth grate with the convulsive action of his jaws; and his face was so ghastly to see that I grew alarmed both for his life and reason.

"Compose yourself," said I.

He turned a dreadful smile to me, and as if with the decision of despair, plucked away the sheet. At sight of the contents, he uttered one loud sob of such immense relief that I sat petrified. And the next moment, in a voice that was already fairly well under control, "Have you a graduated glass?" he asked.

I rose from my place with something of an effort and gave him what he asked.

He thanked me with a smiling nod, measured out a few minims of the red tincture and added one of the powders. The mixture, which was at first of a reddish hue, began, in proportion as the crystals melted, to brighten in colour, to effervesce audibly, and to throw off small fumes of vapour. Suddenly and at the same moment, the ebullition ceased and the compound changed to a dark purple, which faded again more slowly to a watery green. My visitor, who had watched these metamorphoses with a keen eye, smiled, set down the glass upon the table, and then turned and looked upon me with an air of scrutiny.

"And now," said he, "to settle what remains. Will you be wise? Will you be guided? Will you suffer me to take this glass in my hand and to go forth from your house without further parley? Or has the greed of curiosity too much command of you? Think before you answer, for it shall be done as you decide. As you decide, you shall be left as you were before, and neither richer nor wiser, unless the sense of service rendered to a man in mortal distress may be counted as a kind of riches of the soul. Or, if you shall so prefer to choose, a new province of knowledge and new avenues to fame and power shall be laid open to you, here, in this room, upon the instant; and your sight shall be blasted by a prodigy to stagger the unbelief of Satan."

"Sir," said I, affecting a coolness that I was far from truly possessing, "you speak enigmas, and you will perhaps not wonder that I hear you with no very strong impression of belief. But I have gone too far in the way of inexplicable services to pause before I see the end."

"It is well," replied my visitor. "Lanyon, you remember your vows: what follows is under the seal of our profession. And now, you who have so long been bound to the most narrow and material views, you who have denied the virtue of transcendental medicine, you who have derided your superiors—behold!"

He put the glass to his lips and drank at one gulp. A cry

followed; he reeled, staggered, clutched at the table and held on, staring with injected eyes, gasping with open mouth; and as I looked there came, I thought, a change—he seemed to swell—his face became suddenly black and the features seemed to melt and alter—and the next moment, I had sprung to my feet and leaped back against the wall, my arms raised to shield me from that prodigy, my mind submerged in terror.

"O God!" I screamed, and "O God!" again and again; for there before my eyes—pale and shaken, and half fainting, and groping before him with his hands, like a man restored from death—there stood Henry Jekyll!

What he told me in the next hour, I cannot bring my mind to set on paper. I saw what I saw, I heard what I heard, and my soul sickened at it; and yet now when that sight has faded from my eyes, I ask myself if I believe it, and I cannot answer. My life is shaken to its roots; sleep has left me; the deadliest terror sits by me at all hours of the day and night; and I feel that my days are numbered, and that I must die; and yet I shall die incredulous. As for the moral turpitude that man unveiled to me, even with tears of penitence, I cannot, even in memory, dwell on it without a start of horror. I will say but one thing, Utterson, and that (if you can bring your mind to credit it) will be more than enough. The creature who crept into my house that night was, on Jekyll's own confession, known by the name of Hyde and hunted for in every corner of the land as the murderer of Carew.

—HASTIE LANYON

10

HENRY JEKYLL'S FULL STATEMENT OF THE CASE

I WAS BORN in the year 18— to a large fortune, endowed besides with excellent parts, inclined by nature to industry, fond of the respect of the wise and good among my fellow-men, and thus, as might have been supposed, with every guarantee of an honourable and distinguished future. And indeed the worst of my faults was a certain impatient gaiety of disposition, such as has made the happiness of many, but such as I found it hard to reconcile with my imperious desire to carry my head high, and wear a more than commonly grave countenance before the public. Hence it came about that I concealed my pleasures; and that when I reached years of reflection, and began to look round me and take stock of my progress and position in the world, I stood already committed to a profound duplicity of life. Many a man would have even blazoned such irregularities as I was guilty of; but from the high views that I had set before me, I regarded and hid them with an almost morbid sense of shame. It was thus rather the exacting nature of my aspirations than any particular degradation in my faults that made me what I was, and, with even a deeper trench than in the majority of men, severed in me those provinces of good and ill which divide and compound man's dual nature. In this case, I was driven to reflect deeply and inveterately on that hard law of life, which lies at the root of religion and is one of the most plentiful springs of distress. Though so profound a double-dealer, I was in no sense a hypocrite; both sides of me were in dead earnest; I was no more myself when I laid aside restraint and plunged in shame, than when I laboured, in the eye of day, at the futherance of knowledge or the relief of sorrow and suffering. And it chanced that the direction of my scientific studies, which led wholly towards the mystic and the transcendental, reacted and shed a strong light on this consciousness of the perennial war among my members. With every day, and from both sides of my intelligence, the moral and the intellectual, I thus drew steadily nearer to that truth, by whose partial discovery I have been doomed to such a dreadful shipwreck: that man is not truly one, but truly two. I say two, because the state of my own knowledge does not pass beyond that point. Others will follow, others will outstrip me on the same lines; and I hazard the guess that man will be ultimately known for a mere polity of multifarious, incongruous, and independent denizens. I, for my part, from the nature of my life, advanced infallibly in one direction and in one direction only. It was on the moral side, and in my own person, that I learned to recognise the thorough and primitive duality of man; I saw that, of the two natures that contended in the field of my consciousness, even if I could rightly be said to be either, it was only because I was radically both; and from an early date, even before the course of my scientific discoveries had begun to suggest the most naked possibility of such a miracle, I had learned to dwell with pleasure, as a beloved daydream, on the thought of the separation of these elements. If each, I told myself, could be housed in separate identities, life would be relieved of all that was unbearable; the unjust might go his way, delivered from the aspirations and remorse of his more upright twin; and the just could walk steadfastly and securely on his upward path, doing the good things in which he found his pleasure, and no longer exposed to disgrace and penitence by the hands of this extraneous evil. It was the curse of mankind that these incongruous faggots were thus bound together—that in the agonised womb of consciousness, these polar twins should be continuously struggling. How, then were they dissociated?

I was so far in my reflections when, as I have said, a side light began to shine upon the subject from the laboratory table. I began to perceive more deeply than it has ever yet been stated, the trembling immateriality, the mist-like transience, of this seemingly so solid body in which we walk attired. Certain agents I found to have the power to shake and pluck back that fleshly vestment, even as a wind might toss the curtains of a pavilion. For two good reasons, I will not enter deeply into this scientific branch of my confession. First, because I have been made to learn that the doom and burthen of our life is bound forever on man's shoulders, and when the attempt is made to cast it off, it but returns upon us with more unfamiliar and more awful pressure. Second, because, as my narrative will make, alas! too evident, my discoveries were incomplete. Enough then, that I not only recognised my natural body from the mere aura and effulgence of certain of the powers that made up my spirit, but managed to compound a drug by which these powers should be dethroned from their supremacy, and a second form and countenance substituted, none the less natural to me because they were the expression, and bore the stamp of lower elements in my soul.

I hesitated long before I put this theory to the test of practice. I knew well that I risked death; for any drug that so potently controlled and shook the very fortress of identity, might, by the least scruple of an overdose or at the least inopportunity in the moment of exhibition, utterly blot out that immaterial tabernacle which I looked to it to change. But the temptation of a discovery so singular and profound at last overcame the suggestions of alarm. I had long since prepared my tincture; I purchased at once, from a firm of wholesale chemists, a large quantity of a particular salt which I knew, from my experiments, to be the last ingredient required; and late one accursed night, I compounded the elements, watched them boil and smoke together in the glass, and when the ebullition had subsided, with a strong glow of courage, drank off the potion.

The most racking pangs succeeded: a grinding in the bones, deadly nausea, and a horror of the spirit that cannot be exceeded at the hour of birth or death. Then these agonies began swiftly to subside, and I came to myself as if out of a great sickness. There was something strange in my sensations, something indescribably new and, from its very novelty, incredibly sweet. I felt younger, lighter, happier in body; within I was conscious of a heady recklessness, a current of disordered sensual images running like a mill race in my fancy, a solution of the bonds of obligation, an unknown but not an innocent freedom of the soul. I knew myself, at the first breath of this new life, to be more wicked, tenfold more wicked, sold a slave to my original evil; and the thought, in that moment, braced and delighted me like wine. I stretched out my hands, exulting in the freshness of these sensations; and in the act, I was suddenly aware that I had lost in stature.

There was no mirror, at that date, in my room; that which stands beside me as I write, was brought there later on and for the very purpose of these transformations. The night however, was far gone into the morning—the morning, black as it was, was nearly ripe for the conception of the day—the inmates of my house were locked in the most rigorous hours of slumber; and I determined, flushed as I was with hope and triumph, to venture in my new shape as far as to my bedroom. I crossed the yard, wherein the constellations looked down upon me, I could have thought, with wonder, the first creature of that sort that their unsleeping vigilance had yet disclosed to them; I stole through the corridors, a stranger in my own house; and coming to my room, I saw for the first time the appearance of Edward Hyde.

I must here speak by theory alone, saying not that which I know, but that which I suppose to be most probable. The evil side of my nature, to which I had now transferred the stamping efficacy, was less robust and less developed than the good which I had just deposed. Again, in the course of my life, which had been, after all, nine-tenths a life of effort, virtue, and control, it had been much less exercised and much less exhausted. And hence, as I think, it came about that Edward Hyde was so much smaller, slighter, and younger than Henry Jekyll. Even as good shone upon the countenance of the one, evil was written broadly and plainly on the face of the other. Evil besides (which I must still believe to be the lethal side of man) had left on that body an imprint of deformity and decay. And yet when I looked upon that ugly idol in the glass, I was conscious of no repugnance, rather of a leap of welcome. This, too, was myself. It seemed natural and human. In my eyes it bore a livelier image of the spirit, it seemed more express and single, than the imperfect and divided countenance I had been hitherto accustomed to call mine. And in so far I was doubtless right. I have observed that when I wore the semblance of Edward Hyde, none could come near to me at first without a visible misgiving of the flesh. This, as I take it, was because all human beings, as we meet them, are commingled out of good and evil: and Edward Hyde, alone in the ranks of mankind, was pure evil.

I lingered but a moment at the mirror: the second and conclusive experiment had yet to be attempted; it yet remained to be seen if I had lost my identity beyond redemption and must flee before daylight from a house that was no longer mine; and hurrying back to my cabinet, I once more prepared and drank the cup, once more suffered the pangs of dissolution, and came to myself once more with the character, the stature and the face of Henry Jekyll.

That night I had come to the fatal crossroads. Had I approached my discovery in a more noble spirit, had I risked the experiment while under the empire of generous or pious aspirations, all must have been otherwise, and from these agonies of death and birth, I had come forth an angel instead of a fiend. The drug had no discriminating action; it was neither diabolical nor divine; it but shook the doors of the prison-house of my disposition; and like the captives of Philippi, that which stood within ran forth. At that time my virtue slumbered; my evil, kept awake by ambition, was alert and swift to seize the occasion; and the thing that was projected was Edward Hyde. Hence, although I had now two characters as well as two appearances, one was wholly evil, and the other was still the old Henry Jekyll, that incongruous compound of whose reformation and improvement I had already learned to despair. The movement was thus wholly toward the worse.

Even at that time, I had not conquered my aversions to

the dryness of a life of study. I would still be merrily disposed at times; and as my pleasures were (to say the least) undignified, and I was not only well known and highly considered, but growing towards the elderly man, this incoherency of my life was daily growing more unwelcome. It was on this side that my new power tempted me until I fell in slavery. I had but to drink the cup, to doff at once the body of the noted professor, and to assume, like a thick cloak, that of Edward Hyde. I smiled at the notion; it seemed to me at the time to be humorous; and I made my preparations with the most studious care. I took and furnished that house in Soho, to which Hyde was tracked by the police; and engaged as a housekeeper a creature whom I knew well to be silent and unscrupulous. On the other side, I announced to my servants that a Mr. Hyde (whom I described) was to have full liberty and power about my house in the square; and to parry mishaps, I even called and made myself a familiar object, in my second character. I next drew up that will to which you so much objected; so that if anything befell me in the person of Dr. Jekyll, I could enter on that of Edward Hyde without pecuniary loss. And thus fortified, as I supposed, on every side, I began to profit by the strange immunities of my position.

Men have before hired bravos to transact their crimes, while their own person and reputation sat under shelter. I was the first that ever did so for his pleasures. I was the first that could plod in the public eye with a load of genial respectability, and in a moment, like a schoolboy, strip off these lendings and spring headlong into the sea of liberty. But for me, in my impenetrable mantle, the safety was complete. Think of it—I did not even exist! Let me but escape into my laboratory door, give me but a second or two to mix and swallow the draught that I had always standing ready; and whatever he had done, Edward Hyde would pass away like the stain of breath upon a mirror; and there in his stead, quietly at home, trimming the midnight lamp in his study, a man who could afford to laugh at suspicion, would be Henry Jekyll.

The pleasures which I made haste to seek in my disguise were, as I have said, undignified; I would scarce use a harder term. But in the hands of Edward Hyde, they soon began to turn toward the monstrous. When I would come back from these excursions, I was often plunged into a kind of wonder at my vicarious depravity. This familiar that I called out of my own soul, and sent forth alone to do his good pleasure, was a being inherently malign and villainous; his every act and thought centered on self; drinking pleasure with bestial avidity from any degree of torture to another; relentless like a man of stone. Henry Jekyll stood at times aghast before the acts of Edward Hyde; but the situation was apart from ordinary laws, and insidiously relaxed the grasp of conscience. It was Hyde, after all, and Hyde alone, that was guilty. Jekyll was no worse; he woke again to his good qualities seemingly unimpaired; he would even make haste, where it was possible, to undo the evil done by Hyde. And thus his conscience slumbered.

Into the details of the infamy at which I thus connived (for even now I can scarce grant that I committed it) I have no design of entering; I mean but to point out the warnings and the successive steps with which my chastisement approached. I met with one accident which, as it brought on no consequence, I shall no more than mention. An act of cruelty to a child aroused against me the anger of a passerby, whom I recognised the other day in the person of your kinsman; the doctor and the child's family joined him; there were moments when I feared for my life; and at last, in order to pacify their too just resentment, Edward Hyde had to bring them to the door, and pay them in a cheque drawn in the name of Henry Jekyll. But this danger was easily eliminated from the future, by opening an account at another bank in the name of Edward Hyde himself; and when, by sloping my own hand backward, I had supplied my double with a signature, I thought I sat beyond the reach of fate.

Some two months before the murder of Sir Danvers, I had been out for one of my adventures, had returned at a late hour, and woke the next day in bed with somewhat odd sensations. It was in vain I looked about me; in vain I saw the decent furniture and tall proportions of my room in the square; in vain that I recognised the pattern of the bed curtains and the design of the mahogany frame; something still kept insisting that I was not where I was, that I had not wakened where I seemed to be, but in the little room in Soho where I was accustomed to sleep in the body of Edward Hyde. I smiled to myself, and in my psychological way, began lazily to inquire into the elements of this illusion, occasionally, even as I did so, dropping back into a comfortable morning doze. I was still so engaged when, in one of my more wakeful moments, my eyes fell upon my hand. Now the hand of Henry Jekyll (as you have often remarked) was professional in shape and size: it was large, firm, white, and comely. But the hand which I now saw, clearly enough, in the yellow light of a mid-London morning, lying half shut on the bedclothes, was lean, corded, knuckly, of a dusky pallor and thickly shaded with a swart growth of hair. It was the hand of Edward Hyde.

I must have stared upon it for near half a minute, sunk

as I was in the mere stupidity of wonder, before terror woke up in my breast as sudden and startling as the crash of cymbals; and bounding from my bed I rushed to the mirror. At the sight that met my eyes, my blood was changed into something exquisitely thin and icy. Yes, I had gone to bed Henry Jekyll, I had awakened Edward Hyde. How was this to be explained? I asked myself; and then, with another bound of terror—how was it to be remedied? It was well on in the morning; the servants were up; all my drugs were in the cabinet—a long journey down two pairs of stairs, through the back passage, across the open court and through the anatomical theatre, from where I was then standing horror-struck. It might indeed be possible to cover my face; but of what use was that, when I was unable to conceal the alteration in my stature? And then with an overpowering sweetness of relief, it came back upon my mind that the servants were already used to the coming and going of my second self. I had soon dressed, as well as I was able, in clothes of my own size: had soon passed through the house, where Bradshaw stared and drew back at seeing Mr. Hyde at such an hour and in such a strange array; and ten minutes later, Dr. Jekyll had returned to his own shape and was sitting down, with a darkened brow, to make a feint of breakfasting.

Small indeed was my appetite. This inexplicable incident, this reversal of my previous experience, seemed, like the Babylonian finger on the wall, to be spelling out the letters of my judgment; and I began to reflect more seriously than ever before on the issues and possibilities of my double existence. That part of me which I had the power of projecting, had lately been much exercised and nourished; it had seemed to me of late as though the body of Edward

Hyde had grown in stature, as though (when I wore that form) I were conscious of a more generous tide of blood; and I began to spy a danger that, if this were much prolonged, the balance of my nature might be permanently overthrown, the power of voluntary change be forfeited, and the character of Edward Hyde become irrevocably mine. The power of the drug had not been always equally displayed. Once, very early in my career, it had totally failed me; since then I had been obliged on more than one occasion to double, and once, with infinite risk of death, to treble the amount; and these rare uncertainties had cast hitherto the sole shadow on my contentment. Now, however, and in the light of that morning's accident, I was led to remark that whereas, in the beginning, the difficulty had been to throw off the body of Jekyll, it had of late gradually but decidedly transferred itself to the other side. All things therefore seemed to point to this; that I was slowly losing hold of my original and better self, and becoming slowly incorporated with my second and worse.

Between these two, I now felt I had to choose. My two natures had memory in common, but all other faculties were most unequally shared between them. Jekyll (who was composite) now with the most sensitive apprehensions, now with a greedy gusto, projected and shared in the pleasures and adventures of Hyde; but Hyde was indifferent to Jekyll, or but remembered him as the mountain bandit remembers the cavern in which he conceals himself from pursuit. Jekyll had more than a father's interest; Hyde had more than a son's indifference. To cast in my lot with Jekyll, was to die to those appetites which I had long secretly indulged and had of late begun to pamper. To cast it in with Hyde was to die to a thousand interests and aspirations, and to become, at a blow and forever, despised and friendless. The bargain might appear unequal; but there was still another consideration in the scales; for while Jekyll would suffer smartingly in the fires of abstinence, Hyde would be not even conscious of all that he had lost. Strange as my circumstances were, the terms of this debate are as old and commonplace as man; much the same inducements and alarms cast the die for any tempted and trembling sinner; and it fell out with me, as it falls with so vast a majority of my fellows, that I chose the better part and was found wanting in the strength to keep to it.

Yes, I preferred the elderly and discontented doctor, surrounded by friends and cherishing honest hopes; and bade a resolute farewell to the liberty, the comparative youth, the light step, leaping impulses and secret pleasures, that I had enjoyed in the disguise of Hyde. I made this choice perhaps with some unconscious reservation, for I neither gave up the house in Soho, nor destroyed the clothes of Edward Hyde, which still lay ready in my cabinet. For two months, however, I was true to my determination; for two months, I led a life of such severity as I had never before attained to, and enjoyed the compensations of an approving conscience. But time began at last to obliterate the freshness of my alarm; the praises of conscience began to grow into a thing of course; I began to be tortured with throes and longings, as of Hyde struggling after freedom; and at last, in an hour of moral weakness, I once again compounded and swallowed the transforming draught.

I do not suppose that, when a drunkard reasons with himself upon his vice, he is once out of five hundred times affected by the dangers that he runs through his brutish, physical insensibility; neither had I, long as I had considered my position, made enough allowance for the complete moral insensibility and insensate readiness to evil, which were the leading characters of Edward Hyde. Yet it was by these that I was punished. My devil had been long caged, he came out roaring. I was conscious, even when I took the draught, of a more unbridled, a more furious propensity to ill. It must have been this, I suppose, that stirred in my soul that tempest of impatience with which I listened to the civilities of my unhappy victim; I declare, at least, before God, no man morally sane could have been guilty of that crime upon so pitiful a provocation; and that I struck in no more reasonable spirit than that in which a sick child may break a plaything. But I had voluntarily stripped myself of all those balancing instincts by which even the worst of us continues to walk with some degree of steadiness among temptations; and in my case, to be tempted, however slightly, was to fall.

Instantly the spirit of hell awoke in me and raged. With a transport of glee, I mauled the unresisting body, tasting delight from every blow; and it was not till weariness had begun to succeed, that I was suddenly, in the top fit of my delirium, struck through the heart by a cold thrill of terror. A mist dispersed; I saw my life to be forfeit; and fled from the scene of these excesses, at once glorying and trembling, my lust of evil gratified and stimulated, my love of life screwed to the topmost peg. I ran to the house in Soho, and (to make assurance doubly sure) destroyed my papers; thence I set out through the lamplit streets, in the same divided ecstasy of mind, gloating on my crime, light-headedly devising others in the future, and yet still hastening and still hearkening in my wake for the steps of the avenger. Hyde had a song upon his lips as he compounded the draught, and as he drank it, pledged the dead man. The pangs of transformation had not done tearing him, before Henry Jekyll, with streaming tears of gratitude and remorse, had fallen upon his knees and lifted his clasped hands to God. The veil of self-indulgence was rent from head to foot. I saw my life as a whole: I followed it up from the days of childhood, when I had walked with my father's hand, and through the self-denying toils of my professional life, to arrive again and again, with the same sense of unreality, at the damned horrors of the evening. I could have screamed aloud; I sought with tears and prayers to smother down the crowd of hideous images and sounds with which my memory swarmed against me; and still, between the petitions, the ugly face of my iniquity stared into my soul. As the acuteness of this remorse began to die away, it was succeeded by a sense of joy. The problem of my conduct was solved. Hyde was thenceforth impossible; whether I would or not, I was now confined to the better part of my existence; and O, how I rejoiced to think of it! With what willing humility I embraced anew the restrictions of natural life! With what sincere renunciation I locked the door by which I had so often gone and come, and ground the key under my heel!

The next day, came the news that the murder had been overlooked, that the guilt of Hyde was patent to the world, and that the victim was a man high in public estimation. It was not only a crime, it had been a tragic folly. I think I was glad to know it; I think I was glad to have my better impulses thus buttressed and guarded by the terrors of the scaffold. Jekyll was now my city of refuge; let but Hyde peep out an instant, and the hands of all men would be raised to take and slay him.

I resolved in my future conduct to redeem the past; and I can say with honesty that my resolve was fruitful of some good. You know yourself how earnestly, in the last months of the last year, I laboured to relieve suffering; you know that much was done for others, and that the days passed quietly, almost happily for myself. Nor can I truly say that I wearied of this beneficent and innocent life; I think instead that I daily enjoyed it more completely; but I was still cursed with my duality of purpose; and as the first edge of my penitence wore off, the lower side of me, so long indulged, so recently chained down, began to growl for licence. Not that I dreamed of resuscitating Hyde; the bare idea of that would startle me to frenzy: no, it was in my own person that I was once more tempted to trifle with my conscience; and it was as an ordinary secret sinner that I at last fell before the assaults of temptation.

There comes an end to all things; the most capacious measure is filled at last; and this brief condescension to my evil finally destroyed the balance of my soul. And yet I was not alarmed; the fall seemed natural, like a return to the old days before I had made my discovery. It was a fine, clear, January day, wet underfoot where the frost had melted, but cloudless overhead; and the Regent's Park was full of winter chirrupings and sweet with spring odours. I sat in the sun on a bench; the animal within me licking the chops of memory; the spiritual side a little drowsed, promising subsequent penitence, but not yet moved to begin. After all, I reflected, I was like my neighbours; and then I smiled, comparing myself with other men, comparing my active goodwill with the lazy cruelty of their neglect. And at the very moment of that vainglorious thought, a qualm came over me, a horrid nausea and the most deadly shuddering. These passed away, and left me faint; and then as in its turn faintness subsided, I began to be aware of a change in the temper of my thoughts, a greater boldness, a contempt of danger, a solution of the bonds of obligation. I looked down; my clothes hung formlessly on my shrunken limbs; the hand that lay on my knee was corded and hairy. I was once more Edward Hyde. A moment before I had been safe of all men's respect, wealthy, beloved—the cloth laying for me in the dining room at home; and now I was the common quarry of mankind, hunted, houseless, a known murderer, thrall to the gallows.

My reason wavered, but it did not fail me utterly. I have more than once observed that in my second character, my faculties seemed sharpened to a point and my spirits more tensely elastic; thus it came about that, where Jekyll perhaps might have succumbed, Hyde rose to the importance of the moment. My drugs were in one of the presses of my cabinet; how was I to reach them? That was the problem that (crushing my temples in my hands) I set myself to solve. The laboratory door I had closed. If I sought to enter by the house, my own servants would consign me to the gallows. I saw I must employ another hand, and thought of Lanyon. How was he to be reached? How persuaded? Supposing that I escaped capture in the streets, how was I to make my way into his presence? And how should I, an unknown and displeasing visitor, prevail on the famous physician to rifle the study of his colleague, Dr. Jekyll? Then I remembered that of my original character, one part remained to me: I could write my own hand; and once I had conceived that kindling spark, the way that I must follow became lighted up from end to end.

Thereupon, I arranged my clothes as best I could, and summoning a passing hansom, drove to a hotel in Portland Street, the name of which I chanced to remember. At my appearance (which was indeed comical enough, however tragic a fate these garments covered) the driver could not conceal his mirth. I gnashed my teeth upon him with a gust of devilish fury; and the smile withered from his face—happily for him—yet more happily for myself, for in another instant I had certainly dragged him from his perch. At the inn, as I entered, I looked about me with so black a countenance as made the attendants tremble; not a look did they exchange in my presence; but obsequiously took my orders, led me to a private room, and brought me wherewithal to write. Hyde in danger of his life was a creature new to me; shaken with inordinate anger, strung to the pitch of murder, lusting to inflict pain. Yet the creature was astute; mastered his fury with a great effort of the will; composed his two important letters, one to Lanyon and one to Poole; and that he might receive actual evidence of their being posted, sent them out with directions that they should be registered.

Thenceforward, he sat all day over the fire in the private room, gnawing his nails; there he dined, sitting alone with his fears, the waiter visibly quailing before his eye; and thence, when the night was fully come, he set forth in the corner of a closed cab, and was driven to and fro about the streets of the city. He, I say—I cannot say, I. That child of Hell had nothing human; nothing lived in him but fear and hatred. And when at last, thinking the driver had begun to grow suspicious, he discharged the cab and ventured on foot, attired in his misfitting clothes, an object marked out for observation, into the midst of the nocturnal passengers, these two base passions raged within him like a tempest. He walked fast, hunted by his fears, chattering to himself, skulking through the less frequented thoroughfares, counting the minutes that still divided him from midnight. Once a woman spoke to him, offering, I think, a box of lights. He smote her in the face, and she fled.

When I came to myself at Lanyon's, the horror of my old friend perhaps affected me somewhat: I do not know; it was at least but a drop in the sea to the abhorrence with which I looked back upon these hours. A change had come over me. It was no longer the fear of the gallows, it was the horror of being Hyde that racked me. I received Lanyon's condemnation partly in a dream; it was partly in a dream that I came home to my own house and got into bed. I slept after the prostration of the day, with a stringent and profound slumber which not even the nightmares that wrung me could avail to break. I awoke in the morning shaken, weakened, but refreshed. I still hated and feared the thought of the brute that slept within me, and I had not of course forgotten the appalling dangers of the day before; but I was once more at home, in my own house and close to my drugs; and gratitude for my escape shone so strong in my soul that it almost rivalled the brightness of hope.

I was stepping leisurely across the court after breakfast, drinking the chill of the air with pleasure, when I was seized again with those indescribable sensations that heralded the change; and I had but the time to gain the shelter of my cabinet, before I was once again raging and freezing with the passions of Hyde. It took on this occasion a double dose to recall me to myself; and alas! six hours after, as I sat looking sadly in the fire, the pangs returned, and the drug had to be re-administered. In short, from that day forth it seemed only by a great effort as of gymnastics, and only under the immediate stimulation of the drug, that I was able to wear the countenance of Jekyll. At all hours of the day and night, I would be taken with the premonitory shudder; above all, if I slept, or even dozed for a moment in my chair, it was always as Hyde that I awakened. Under the strain of this continually impending doom and by the sleeplessness to which I now condemned myself, ay, even beyond what I had thought possible to man, I became, in my own person, a creature eaten up and emptied by fever, languidly weak both in body and mind, and solely occupied by one thought: the horror of my other self. But when I slept, or when the virtue of the medicine wore off, I would leap almost without transition (for the pangs of transformation grew daily less marked) into the possession of a fancy brimming with images of terror, a soul boiling with causeless hatreds, and a body that seemed not strong enough to contain the raging energies of life. The powers of Hyde seemed to have grown with the sickliness of Jekyll. And certainly the hate that now divided them was equal on each side. With Jekyll, it was a thing of vital instinct. He had now seen the full deformity of that creature that shared with him some of the phenomena of consciousness, and was co-heir with him to death: and beyond these links of community, which in themselves made the most poignant part of his distress, he thought of Hyde, for all his energy of life, as of something not only hellish but inorganic. This was the shocking thing; that the slime of the pit seemed to utter cries and voices; that the amorphous dust gesticulated and sinned; that what was dead, and had no shape, should usurp the offices of life. And this again, that that insurgent horror was knit to him closer than a wife, closer than an eye; lay caged in his flesh, where he heard it mutter and felt it struggle to be born; and at every hour of weakness, and in the confidence of slumber, prevailed against him, and deposed him out of life. The hatred of Hyde for Jekyll was of a different order. His terror of the gallows drove him continually to commit temporary suicide, and return to his subordinate station of a part instead of a person; but he loathed the necessity, he loathed the despondency into which Jekyll was now fallen, and he resented the dislike with which he was himself regarded. Hence the ape-like tricks that he would play me, scrawling in my own hand blasphemies on the pages of my books, burning the letters and destroying the portrait of my father; and indeed, had it not been for his fear of death, he would long ago have ruined himself in order to involve me in the ruin. But his love of me is wonderful; I go further: I, who sicken and freeze at the mere thought of him, when I recall the abjection and passion of this attachment, and when I know how he fears my power to cut him off by suicide, I find it in my heart to pity him.

It is useless, and the time awfully fails me, to prolong this description; no one has ever suffered such torments, let that suffice; and yet even to these, habit brought—no, not alleviation—but a certain callousness of soul, a certain acquiescence of despair; and my punishment might have gone on for years, but for the last calamity which has now fallen, and which has finally severed me from my own face and nature. My provision of the salt, which had never been renewed since the date of the first experiment, began to run low. I sent out for a fresh supply and mixed the draught; the ebullition followed, and the first change of colour, not the second; I drank it and it was without efficiency. You will learn from Poole how I have had London ransacked; it was in vain; and I am now persuaded that my first supply was impure, and that it was that unknown impurity which lent efficacy to the draught.

About a week has passed, and I am now finishing this statement under the influence of the last of the old powders. This, then, is the last time, short of a miracle, that Henry Jekyll can think his own thoughts or see his own face (now how sadly altered!) in the glass. Nor must I delay too long to bring my writing to an end; for if my narrative has hitherto escaped destruction, it has been by a combination of great prudence and great good luck. Should the throes of change take me in the act of writing it, Hyde will tear it in pieces; but if some time shall have elapsed after I have laid it by, his wonderful selfishness and circumscription to the moment will probably save it once again from the action of his ape-like spite. And indeed the doom that is closing on us both has already changed and crushed him. Half an hour from now, when I shall again and forever reindue that hated personality, I know how I shall sit shuddering and weeping in my chair, or continue, with the most strained and fear-struck ecstasy of listening, to pace up and down this room (my last earthly refuge) and give ear to every sound of menace. Will Hyde die upon the scaffold? Or will he find courage to release himself at the last moment? God knows; I am careless; this is my true hour of death, and what is to follow concerns another than myself. Here then, as I lay down the pen and proceed to seal up my confession, I bring the life of that unhappy Henry Jekyll to an end.

SPARKNOTES™

Reader's Companion

CONTENTS

Context

ROBERT LOUIS STEVENSON, one of the masters of the Victorian adventure story, was born in Edinburgh, Scotland, on November 13, 1850. He was a sickly child, and respiratory troubles plagued him throughout his life. As a young man, he traveled through Europe, leading a bohemian lifestyle and penning his first two books, both travel narratives. In 1876, he met a married woman, Fanny Van de Grift Osbourne, and fell in love with her. Mrs. Osbourne eventually divorced her husband, and she and Stevenson were married.

Stevenson returned to London with his bride and wrote prolifically over the next decade, in spite of his terrible health. He won widespread admiration with *Treasure Island,* written in 1883, and followed it with *Kidnapped* in 1886; both were adventure stories, the former a pirate tale set on the high seas and the latter a historical novel set in Stevenson's native Scotland. *Dr. Jekyll and Mr. Hyde,* which Stevenson described as a "fine bogey tale," also came out in 1886. It met with tremendous success, selling 40,000 copies in six months and ensuring Stevenson's fame as a writer.

In its narrative of a respectable doctor who transforms himself into a savage murderer, *Dr. Jekyll and Mr. Hyde* tapped directly into the anxieties of Stevenson's age. The Victorian era, named for Queen Victoria, who ruled England for most of the nineteenth century, was a time of unprecedented technological progress and an age in which European nations carved up the world with their empires. By the end of the century, however, many people were beginning to call into question the ideals of progress and civilization that had defined the era, and a growing sense of pessimism and decline pervaded artistic circles. Many felt that the end of the century was also witnessing a twilight of Western culture.

With the notion of a single body containing both the erudite Dr. Jekyll and the depraved Mr. Hyde, Stevenson's novel imagines an inextricable link between civilization and savagery, good and evil. Jekyll's attraction to the freedom from restraint that Hyde enjoys mirrors Victorian England's secret attraction to allegedly savage non-Western cultures, even as Europe claimed superiority over them. This attraction also informs such books as Joseph Conrad's *Heart of Darkness.* For, as the Western world came in contact with other peoples and ways of life, it found aspects of these cultures within itself, and both desired and feared to indulge them. These aspects included open sensuality, physicality, and other so-called irrational tendencies. Even as Victorian England sought to assert its civilization over and against these instinctual sides of life, it found them secretly fascinating. Indeed, society's repression of its darker side only increased the fascination. As a product of this society, *Dr. Jekyll and Mr. Hyde* manifests this fascination; yet, as a work of art, it also questions this interest.

By the late 1880s, Stevenson had become one of the leading lights of English literature. But even after garnering fame, he led a somewhat troubled life. He traveled often, seeking to find a climate more amenable to the tuberculosis that haunted his later days. Eventually he settled in Samoa, and there Stevenson died suddenly in 1894, at the age of forty-four.

Plot Overview

ON THEIR WEEKLY walk, an eminently sensible, trustworthy lawyer named Mr. Utterson listens as his friend Enfield tells a gruesome tale of assault. The tale describes a sinister figure named Mr. Hyde who tramples a young girl, disappears into a door on the street, and reemerges to pay off her relatives with a check signed by a respectable gentleman. Since both Utterson and Enfield disapprove of gossip, they agree to speak no further of the matter. It happens, however, that one of Utterson's clients and close friends, Dr. Jekyll, has written a will transferring all of his property to this same Mr. Hyde. Soon, Utterson begins having dreams in which a faceless figure stalks through a nightmarish version of London.

Puzzled, the lawyer visits Jekyll and their mutual friend Dr. Lanyon to try to learn more. Lanyon reports that he no longer sees much of Jekyll, since they had a dispute over the course of Jekyll's research, which Lanyon calls "unscientific balderdash." Curious, Utterson stakes out a building that Hyde visits—which, it turns out, is a laboratory attached to the back of Jekyll's home. Encountering Hyde, Utterson is amazed by how undefinably ugly the man seems, as if deformed, though Utterson cannot say exactly how. Much to Utterson's surprise, Hyde willingly offers Utterson his address. Jekyll tells Utterson not to concern himself with the matter of Hyde.

A year passes uneventfully. Then, one night, a servant girl witnesses Hyde brutally beat to death an old man named Sir Danvers Carew, a member of Parliament and a client of Utterson. The police contact Utterson, and Utterson suspects Hyde as the murderer. He leads the officers to Hyde's apartment, feeling a sense of foreboding amid the eerie weather—the morning is dark and wreathed in fog. When they arrive at the apartment, the murderer has vanished, and police searches prove futile. Shortly thereafter, Utterson again visits Jekyll, who now claims to have ended all relations with Hyde; he shows Utterson a note, allegedly written to Jekyll by Hyde, apologizing for the trouble he has caused him and saying goodbye. That night, however, Utterson's clerk points out that Hyde's handwriting bears a remarkable similarity to Jekyll's own.

For a few months, Jekyll acts especially friendly and sociable, as if a weight has been lifted from his shoulders. But then Jekyll suddenly begins to refuse visitors, and Lanyon dies from some kind of shock he received in connection with Jekyll. Before dying, however, Lanyon gives Utterson a letter, with instructions that he not open it until after Jekyll's death. Meanwhile, Utterson goes out walking with Enfield, and they see Jekyll at a window of his laboratory; the three men begin to converse, but a look of horror comes over Jekyll's face, and he slams the window and disappears. Soon afterward, Jekyll's butler, Mr. Poole, visits Utterson in a state of desperation: Jekyll has secluded himself in his laboratory for several weeks, and now the voice that comes from the room sounds nothing like the doctor's. Utterson and Poole travel to Jekyll's house through empty, windswept, sinister streets; once there, they find the servants huddled together in fear. After arguing for a time, the two of them resolve to break into Jekyll's laboratory. Inside, they find the body of Hyde, wearing Jekyll's clothes and apparently dead by suicide—and a letter from Jekyll to Utterson promising to explain everything.

Utterson takes the document home, where first he reads

Lanyon's letter; it reveals that Lanyon's deterioration and eventual death were caused by the shock of seeing Mr. Hyde take a potion and metamorphose into Dr. Jekyll. The second letter constitutes a testament by Jekyll. It explains how Jekyll, seeking to separate his good side from his darker impulses, discovered a way to transform himself periodically into a deformed monster free of conscience—Mr. Hyde. At first, Jekyll reports, he delighted in becoming Hyde and rejoiced in the moral freedom that the creature possessed. Eventually, however, he found that he was turning into Hyde involuntarily in his sleep, even without taking the potion. At this point, Jekyll resolved to cease becoming Hyde. One night, however, the urge gripped him too strongly, and after the transformation he immediately rushed out and violently killed Sir Danvers Carew. Horrified, Jekyll tried more adamantly to stop the transformations, and for a time he proved successful; one day, however, while sitting in a park, he suddenly turned into Hyde, the first time that an involuntary metamorphosis had happened while he was awake.

The letter continues describing Jekyll's cry for help. Far from his laboratory and hunted by the police as a murderer, Hyde needed Lanyon's help to get his potions and become Jekyll again—but when he undertook the transformation in Lanyon's presence, the shock of the sight instigated Lanyon's deterioration and death. Meanwhile, Jekyll returned to his home, only to find himself ever more helpless and trapped as the transformations increased in frequency and necessitated even larger doses of potion in order to reverse themselves. It was the onset of one of these spontaneous metamorphoses that caused Jekyll to slam his laboratory window shut in the middle of his conversation with Enfield and Utterson. Eventually, the potion began to run out, and Jekyll was unable to find a key ingredient to make more. His ability to change back from Hyde into Jekyll slowly vanished. Jekyll writes that even as he composes his letter he knows that he will soon become Hyde permanently, and he wonders if Hyde will face execution for his crimes or choose to kill himself. Jekyll notes that, in any case, the end of his letter marks the end of the life of Dr. Jekyll. With these words, both the document and the novel come to a close.

Character List

Dr. Henry Jekyll

A respected doctor and friend of both Lanyon, a fellow physician, and Utterson, a lawyer. Jekyll is a seemingly prosperous man, well established in the community, and known for his decency and charitable works. Since his youth, however, he has secretly engaged in unspecified dissolute and corrupt behavior. Jekyll finds this dark side a burden and undertakes experiments intended to separate his good and evil selves from one another. Through these experiments, he brings Mr. Hyde into being, finding a way to transform himself in such a way that he fully becomes his darker half.

Mr. Edward Hyde

A strange, repugnant man who looks faintly prehuman. Hyde is violent and cruel, and everyone who sees him describes him as ugly and deformed—yet no one can say exactly why. Language itself seems to fail around Hyde: he is not a creature who belongs to the rational world, the world of conscious articulation or logical grammar. Hyde is Jekyll's dark side, released from the bonds of conscience and loosed into the world by a mysterious potion.

Mr. Gabriel John Utterson

A prominent and upstanding lawyer, well respected in the London community. Utterson is reserved, dignified, and perhaps even lacking somewhat in imagination, but he does seem to possess a furtive curiosity about the more sordid side of life. His rationalism, however, makes him ill equipped to deal with the supernatural nature of the Jekyll-Hyde connection. While not a man of science, Utterson resembles his friend Dr. Lanyon—and perhaps Victorian society at large—in his devotion to reasonable explanations and his denial of the supernatural.

Dr. Hastie Lanyon

A reputable London doctor and, along with Utterson, formerly one of Jekyll's closest friends. As an embodiment of rationalism, materialism, and skepticism, Lanyon serves a foil (a character whose attitudes or emotions contrast with, and thereby illuminate, those of another character) for Jekyll, who embraces mysticism. His death represents the more general victory of supernaturalism over materialism in *Dr. Jekyll and Mr. Hyde.*

Mr. Poole

Jekyll's butler. Mr. Poole is a loyal servant, having worked for the doctor for twenty years, and his concern for his master eventually drives him to seek Utterson's help when he becomes convinced that something has happened to Jekyll.

Mr. Enfield

A distant cousin and lifelong friend of Mr. Utterson. Like Utterson, Enfield is reserved, formal, and scornful of gossip; indeed, the two men often walk together for long stretches without saying a word to one another.

Mr. Guest

Utterson's clerk and confidant. Guest is also an expert in handwriting. His skill proves particularly useful when Utterson wants him to examine a bit of Hyde's handwriting. Guest notices that Hyde's script is the same as Jekyll's, but slanted the other way.

Sir Danvers Carew

A well-liked old nobleman, a member of Parliament, and a client of Utterson.

Analysis of Major Characters

DR. JEKYLL & MR. HYDE

One might question the extent to which Dr. Jekyll and Mr. Hyde are in fact a single character. Until the end of the novel, the two personas seem nothing alike—the well-liked, respectable doctor and the hideous, depraved Hyde are almost opposite in type and personality. Stevenson uses this marked contrast to make his point: every human being contains opposite forces within him or her, an alter ego that hides behind one's polite facade. Correspondingly, to understand fully the significance of either Jekyll or Hyde, we must ultimately consider the two as constituting one single character. Indeed, taken alone, neither is a very interesting personality; it is the nature of their interrelationship that gives the novel its power.

Despite the seeming diametric opposition between Dr. Jekyll and Mr. Hyde, their relationship in fact involves a complicated dynamic. While it is true that Jekyll largely appears as moral and decent, engaging in charity work and enjoying a reputation as a courteous and genial man, he in fact never fully embodies virtue in the way that Hyde embodies evil. Although Jekyll undertakes his experiments with the intent of purifying his good side from his bad and vice versa, he ends up separating the bad alone, while leaving his former self, his Jekyll-self, as mixed as before. Jekyll succeeds in liberating his darker side, freeing it from the bonds of conscience, yet as Jekyll he never liberates himself from this darkness.

Jekyll's partial success in his endeavors warrants much

analysis. Jekyll himself ascribes his lopsided results to his state of mind when first taking the potion. He says that he was motivated by dark urges such as ambition and pride when he first drank the liquid and that these allowed for the emergence of Hyde. He seems to imply that, had he entered the experiment with pure motives, an angelic being would have emerged. However, one must consider the subsequent events in the novel before acquitting Jekyll of any blame. For, once released, Hyde gradually comes to dominate both personas, until Jekyll takes Hyde's shape more often than his own. Indeed, by the very end of the novel, Jekyll himself no longer exists and only Hyde remains. Hyde seems to possess a force more powerful than Jekyll originally believed. The fact that Hyde, rather than some beatific creature, emerged from Jekyll's experiments seems more than a chance event, subject to an arbitrary state of mind. Rather, Jekyll's drinking of the potion seems almost to have afforded Hyde the opportunity to assert himself. It is as if Hyde, but no comparable virtuous essence, was lying in wait.

This dominance of Hyde—first as a latent force within Jekyll, then as a tyrannical external force subverting Jekyll—holds various implications for our understanding of human nature. We begin to wonder whether any aspect of human nature in fact stands as a counter to an individual's Hyde-like side. We may recall that Hyde is described as "troglodytic," like a primitive creature; perhaps Hyde is actually the original, authentic nature of man, which has been repressed but not destroyed by the accumulated weight of civilization, conscience, and societal norms. Perhaps man doesn't have two natures but rather a single, primitive, amoral one that remains just barely constrained by the bonds of civilization. Moreover, the novel suggests that once those bonds are broken, it becomes impossible to reestablish them; the genie cannot be put back into the bottle, and eventually Hyde will permanently replace Jekyll—as he finally does. Even in Victorian England—which considered itself the height of Western civilization—Stevenson suggests that the dark, instinctual side of man remains strong enough to devour anyone who, like Jekyll, proves foolish enough to unleash it.

MR. GABRIEL JOHN UTTERSON

Although Utterson witnesses a string of shocking events, Utterson himself is a largely unexciting character and is clearly not a man of strong passions or sensibilities. Indeed, Stevenson intends for him to come across in this way: from the first page of the novel, the text notes that Utterson has a face that is "never lighted by a smile," that he speaks very little, and that he seems "lean, long, dusty, [and] dreary." Yet, somehow, he is also "lovable," and dull and proper though he may be, he has many friends. His lovability may stem from the only interesting quality that Stevenson gives him—namely, his willingness to remain friends with someone whose reputation has suffered. This loyalty leads him to plumb the mystery that surrounds Jekyll.

Utterson represents the perfect Victorian gentleman. He consistently seeks to preserve order and decorum, does not gossip, and guards his friends' reputations as though they were his own. Even when he suspects his friend Jekyll of criminal activities such as blackmail or the sheltering of a murderer, he prefers to sweep what he has learned—or what he thinks he has learned—under the rug rather than bring ruin upon his good friend.

Utterson's status as the epitome of Victorian norms also

stems from his devotion to reason and common sense. He investigates what becomes a supernatural sequence of events but never allows himself to even entertain the notion that something uncanny may be going on. He considers that misdeeds may be occurring but not that the mystical or metaphysical might be afoot. Thus, even at the end, when he is summoned by Poole to Jekyll's home and all the servants are gathered frightened in the hallway, Utterson continues to look for an explanation that preserves reason. He desperately searches for excuses not to take any drastic steps to interfere with Jekyll's life. In Utterson's devotion to both decorum and reason, Stevenson depicts Victorian society's general attempt to maintain the authority of civilization over and against humanity's darker side. Stevenson suggests that just as Utterson prefers the suppression or avoidance of revelations to the scandal or chaos that the truth might unleash, so too does Victorian society prefer to repress and deny the existence of an uncivilized or savage element of humanity, no matter how intrinsic that element may be.

Yet, even as Utterson adheres rigidly to order and rationality, he does not fail to notice the uncanny quality of the events he investigates. Indeed, because we see the novel through Utterson's eyes, Stevenson cannot allow Utterson to be *too* unimaginative—otherwise the novel's eerie mood would suffer. Correspondingly, Stevenson attributes nightmares to Utterson and grants him ominous premonitions as he moves through the city at night—neither of which seem to suit the lawyer's normally reasonable personality, which is rarely given to flights of fancy. Perhaps, the novel suggests, the chilling presence of Hyde in London is strong enough to penetrate even the rigidly rational shell that surrounds Utterson, planting a seed of supernatural dread.

DR. HASTIE LANYON

Lanyon plays only a minor role in the novel's plot, but his thematic significance extends beyond his brief appearances. When we first encounter him, he speaks dismissively of Jekyll's experiments, referring to them as "unscientific balderdash." His scientific skepticism renders him, to an even greater extent than Utterson, an embodiment of rationalism and a proponent of materialist explanations. As such, he functions as a kind of foil for Jekyll. Both men are doctors, well respected and successful, but they have chosen divergent paths. From Lanyon's early remarks, we learn that Jekyll shared some of his research with Lanyon, and one may even imagine that they were partners at one point. But Lanyon chooses to engage in rational, materialist science, while Jekyll prefers to pursue what might be called mystical or metaphysical science.

It is appropriate, then, that Lanyon is the first person to see Jekyll enact his transformations—the great advocate of material causes is witness to undeniable proof of a metaphysical, physically impossible phenomenon. Having spent his life as a rationalist and a skeptic, Lanyon cannot deal with the world that Jekyll's experiments have revealed. Deep within himself, Lanyon prefers to die rather than go on living in a universe that, from his point of view, has been turned upside down. After his cataclysmic experience, Lanyon, who has spent his life pursuing knowledge, explicitly rejects the latest knowledge he has gained. "I sometimes think if we knew all," he tells Utterson, "we should be more glad to get away." With these words, Lanyon departs from the novel, his uncompromising rationalism ceding to the inexplicable reality of Jekyll.

Themes, Motifs & Symbols

THEMES

Themes are the fundamental and often universal ideas explored in a literary work.

THE DUALITY OF HUMAN NATURE

Dr. Jekyll and Mr. Hyde centers upon a conception of humanity as dual in nature, although the theme does not emerge fully until the last chapter, when the complete story of the Jekyll-Hyde relationship is revealed. Therefore, we confront the theory of a dual human nature explicitly only after having witnessed all of the events of the novel, including Hyde's crimes and his ultimate eclipsing of Jekyll. The text not only posits the duality of human nature as its central theme but forces us to ponder the properties of this duality and to consider each of the novel's episodes as we weigh various theories.

Jekyll asserts that "man is not truly one, but truly two," and he imagines the human soul as the battleground for an "angel" and a "fiend," each struggling for mastery. But his potion, which he hoped would separate and purify each element, succeeds only in bringing the dark side into being—Hyde emerges, but he has no angelic counterpart. Once unleashed, Hyde slowly takes over, until Jekyll ceases to exist. If man is half angel and half fiend, one wonders what happens to the "angel" at the end of the novel.

Perhaps the angel gives way permanently to Jekyll's devil. Or perhaps Jekyll is simply mistaken: man is not "truly two" but is first and foremost the primitive creature embodied in Hyde, brought under tentative control by civilization, law, and conscience. According to this theory, the potion simply strips away the civilized veneer, exposing man's essential nature. Certainly, the novel goes out of its way to paint Hyde as animalistic—he is hairy and ugly; he conducts himself according to instinct rather than reason; Utterson describes him as "troglodytic," comparing him to a primitive creature.

Yet if Hyde were just an animal, we would not expect him to take such *delight* in crime. Indeed, he seems to commit violent acts against innocents for no reason except the joy of it—something that no animal would do. He appears deliberately and happily *im*moral rather than *a*moral; he knows the moral law and basks in his breach of it. For an animalistic creature, furthermore, Hyde seems oddly at home in the urban landscape. All of these observations imply that perhaps civilization, too, has its dark side.

Ultimately, while Stevenson clearly asserts human nature as possessing two aspects, he leaves open the question of what these aspects constitute. Perhaps they consist of evil and virtue; perhaps they represent one's inner animal and the veneer that civilization has imposed. Stevenson enhances the richness of the novel by leaving us to look within ourselves to find the answers.

THE IMPORTANCE OF REPUTATION

For the characters in *Dr. Jekyll and Mr. Hyde,* preserving one's reputation emerges as all important. The prevalence of this value system is evident in the way that upright men such as Utterson and Enfield avoid gossip at all costs; they see gossip as a great destroyer of reputation. Similarly, when Utterson suspects Jekyll first of being blackmailed and then of sheltering Hyde from the police, he does not make his suspicions known; part of being Jekyll's good friend is a willingness to keep his secrets and not ruin his respectability. The importance of reputation in the novel also reflects the importance of appearances, facades, and surfaces, which often hide a sordid underside. In many instances in the novel, Utterson, true to his Victorian society, adamantly wishes not only to preserve Jekyll's reputation but also to preserve the appearance of order and decorum, even as he senses a vile truth lurking underneath.

MOTIFS

Motifs are recurring structures, contrasts, or literary devices that can help to develop and inform the text's major themes.

VIOLENCE AGAINST INNOCENTS

The text repeatedly depicts Hyde as a creature of great evil and countless vices. Although the reader learns the details of only two of Hyde's crimes, the nature of both underlines his depravity. Both involve violence directed against innocents in particular. In the first instance, the victim of Hyde's violence is a small, female child; in the second instance, it is a gentle and much-beloved old man. The fact that Hyde ruthlessly assaults these harmless beings, who have seemingly done nothing to provoke his rage, emphasizes the extreme immorality of Jekyll's dark side unleashed. Hyde's brand of evil constitutes not just a lapse from good but an outright attack on it.

SILENCE

Repeatedly in the novel, characters fail or refuse to articulate themselves. Either they seem unable to describe a horrifying perception, such as the physical characteristics of Hyde, or they deliberately abort or avoid certain conversations. Enfield and Utterson cut off their discussion of Hyde in the first chapter out of a distaste for gossip; Utterson refuses to share his suspicions about Jekyll throughout his investigation of his client's predicament. Moreover, neither Jekyll in his final confession nor the third-person narrator in the rest of the novel ever provides any details of Hyde's sordid behavior and secret vices. It is unclear whether these narrative silences owe to a failure of language or a refusal to use it.

Ultimately, the two kinds of silence in the novel indicate two different notions about the interaction of the rational and the irrational. The characters' refusals to discuss the sordid indicate an attribute of the Victorian society in which they live. This society prizes decorum and reputation above all and prefers to repress or even deny the truth if that truth threatens to upset the conventionally ordered worldview. Faced with the irrational, Victorian society and its inhabitants prefer not to acknowledge its presence and not to grant it the legitimacy of a name. Involuntary silences, on the other hand, imply something about language itself. Language is by nature rational and logical, a method by which we map and delineate our world. Perhaps when confronted with the irrational and the mystical, language itself simply breaks down. Perhaps something about verbal expression stands at odds with the supernatural. Interestingly, certain parts of the novel suggest that, in the clash between language and the uncanny, the uncanny need not always win. One can interpret Stevenson's reticence on the topic of Jekyll and Hyde's crimes as a conscious choice not to defuse their chilling aura with descriptions that might only dull them.

URBAN TERROR

Throughout the novel, Stevenson goes out of his way to establish a link between the urban landscape of Victorian London and the dark events surrounding Hyde. He achieves his desired effect through the use of nightmarish imagery, in which dark streets twist and coil, or lie draped in fog, forming a sinister landscape befitting the crimes that take place there. Chilling visions of the city appear in Utterson's nightmares as well, and the text notes that

> He would be aware of the great field of lamps of a nocturnal city. . . . The figure [of Hyde] . . . haunted the lawyer all night; and if at any time he dozed over, it was but to see it glide more stealthily through sleeping houses, or move the more swiftly . . . through wider labyrinths of lamplighted city, and at every street corner crush a child and leave her screaming.

In such images, Stevenson paints Hyde as an urban creature, utterly at home in the darkness of London—where countless crimes take place, the novel suggests, without anyone knowing.

SYMBOLS

Symbols are objects, characters, figures, or colors used to represent abstract ideas or concepts.

JEKYLL'S HOUSE AND LABORATORY

Dr. Jekyll lives in a well-appointed home, characterized by Stevenson as having "a great air of wealth and comfort." His laboratory is described as "a certain sinister block of building . . . [which] bore in every feature the marks of profound and sordid negligence." With its decaying facade and air of neglect, the laboratory quite neatly symbolizes the corrupt and perverse Hyde. Correspondingly, the respectable, prosperous-looking main house symbolizes the respectable, upright Jekyll. Moreover, the connection between the buildings similarly corresponds to the connection between the personas they represent. The buildings are adjoined but look out on two different streets. Because of the convoluted layout of the streets in the area, the casual observer cannot detect that the structures are two parts of a whole, just as he or she would be unable to detect the relationship between Jekyll and Hyde.

HYDE'S PHYSICAL APPEARANCE

According to the indefinite remarks made by his overwhelmed observers, Hyde appears repulsively ugly and deformed, small, shrunken, and hairy. His physical ugliness and deformity symbolizes his moral hideousness and warped ethics. Indeed, for the audience of Stevenson's time, the connection between such ugliness and Hyde's wickedness might have been seen as more than symbolic. Many people believed in the science of physiognomy, which held that one could identify a criminal by physical appearance. Additionally, Hyde's small stature may represent the fact that, as Jekyll's dark side, he has been repressed for years, prevented from growing and flourishing. His hairiness may indicate that he is not so much an evil side of Jekyll as the embodiment of Jekyll's instincts, the animalistic core beneath Jekyll's polished exterior.

Summary & Analysis

CHAPTER 1: "STORY OF THE DOOR"

SUMMARY

> *Mr. Utterson the lawyer was a man of a rugged countenance . . . the last good influence in the lives of down-going men.*
>
> (See Quotations, p. 149)

Mr. Utterson is a wealthy, well-respected London lawyer, a reserved and perhaps even boring man who nevertheless inspires a strange fondness in those who know him. Despite his eminent respectability, he never abandons a friend whose reputation has been sullied or ruined.

Utterson nurtures a close friendship with Mr. Enfield, his distant relative and likewise a respectable London gentleman. The two seem to have little in common, and when they take their weekly walk together they often go for quite a distance without saying anything to one another; nevertheless, they look forward to these strolls as one of the high points of the week.

As the story begins, Utterson and Enfield are taking their regular Sunday stroll and walking down a particularly prosperous-looking street. They come upon a neglected building, which seems out of place in the neighborhood, and Enfield relates a story in connection with it. Enfield was walking in the same neighborhood late one night, when he witnessed a shrunken, misshapen man crash into and trample a young girl. He collared the man before he could get away, and then brought him back to the girl, around whom an angry crowd had gathered. The captured man appeared so overwhelmingly ugly that the crowd immediately despised him. United, the crowd threatened to ruin the ugly man's good name unless he did something to make amends; the man, seeing himself trapped, bought them off with one hundred pounds, which he obtained upon entering the neglected building through its only door. Strangely enough, the check bore the name of a very reputable man; furthermore, and in spite of Enfield's suspicions, it proved to be legitimate and not a forgery. Enfield hypothesizes that the ugly culprit had somehow blackmailed the man whose name appeared on the check. Spurning gossip, however, Enfield refuses to reveal that name.

Utterson then asks several pointed questions confirming the details of the incident. Enfield tries to describe the nature of the mysterious man's ugliness but cannot express it, stating, "I never saw a man I so disliked, and yet I scarce know why." He divulges that the culprit's name was Hyde, and, at this point, Utterson declares that he knows the man, and notes that he can now guess the name on the check. But, as the men have just been discussing the virtue of minding one's own business, they promptly agree never to discuss the matter again.

> *He is not easy to describe. . . . And it's not want of memory; for I declare I can see him this moment.*
>
> (See Quotations, p. 150)

ANALYSIS

The story of Jekyll and Hyde is one of the most well known in the English language, and few readers come to this novel without knowing the secret behind the relationship of the title characters. Nevertheless, it is important to remember that Stevenson's novel does not reveal this secret until the very end. Instead, the book presents us with what seems like a detective novel, beginning with a sinister figure of unknown origin, a mysterious act of violence, and hints of blackmail and secret scandal. Although the opening scene also contains vaguely supernatural elements, particularly in the strange dread that Hyde inspires, Stevenson likely intended his readers to enter the novel believing it to be nothing more than a mystery story. The uncanny side of the novel appears gradually, as Utterson's detective work leads him toward the seemingly impossible truth.

Even as it plunges us into the mysterious happenings surrounding Mr. Hyde, the first chapter highlights the proper, respectable, eminently Victorian attitudes of Enfield and Utterson. The text describes these men as reserved—so reserved, in fact, that they can enjoy a lengthy walk during which neither man says a word. Declining to indulge their more impulsive thoughts and feelings, they display a mutual distaste for sensation and gossip. They steer away from discussing the matter of Hyde once they realize it involves someone Utterson knows. The Victorian value system largely privileged reputation over reality, and this prioritization is reflected both in the narrator's remarks about Utterson and Enfield and in the characters' own remarks about gossip and blackmail. In a society so focused on reputation, blackmail proves a particularly potent force, since those possessing and concerned with good reputations will do anything they can to preserve them. Thus, when Hyde tramples the little girl, Enfield and the crowd can blackmail him into paying off her family; Hyde's access to a respectable man's bank account leads Enfield to leap to the conclusion that Hyde is blackmailing his benefactor.

In such a society, it is significant that Utterson, so

respectable himself, is known for his willingness to remain friends with people whose reputations have been damaged, or ruined. This aspect of his personality suggests not only a sense of charity, but also hints that Utterson is intrigued, in some way, by the darker side of the world—the side that the truly respectable, like Enfield, carefully avoid. It is this curiosity on Utterson's part that leads him to investigate the peculiar figure of Mr. Hyde rather than avoid looking into matters that could touch on scandal.

However, while Utterson may take an interest in affairs that polite society would like to ignore, he remains a steadfast rationalist and a fundamentally unimaginative man without a superstitious bone in his body. One of the central themes of the novel is the clash between Victorian rationalism and the supernatural, and Utterson emerges as the embodiment of this rationality, always searching out the logical explanation for events and deliberately dismissing supernatural flights of fancy. Enfield approaches the world in much the same way, serving as another representative of the commonsense approach. By allowing these men and their Victorian perspectives to dominate the novel's point of view, Stevenson proves better able to dramatize the opposition between the rationalism that they represent and the fantastical subject matter that comes under scrutiny in this focus. However, while this method contributes much to the story's overall effect, it also presents a challenge for Stevenson. The author must struggle to convey to us a sense of metaphysical dread surrounding Hyde, even as he situates his novel's viewpoint with men who never feel such emotions themselves.

In the opening chapter, Stevenson overcomes this challenge by highlighting his characters' inability to express and come to terms with the events that they have witnessed.

"There is something wrong with [Hyde's] appearance," Enfield says. "I never saw a man I so disliked, and yet I scarce know why. He must be deformed somewhere; he gives a strong feeling of deformity, although I couldn't specify the point." In other words, Hyde's ugliness is not physical but metaphysical; it attaches to his soul more than to his body. Enfield and, later, Utterson, whose minds are not suited to the metaphysical, can sense Hyde's uncanniness but cannot describe it. Their limited imaginations fail them as they approach the eerie and inexplicable; as rational clashes with irrational, language breaks down.

CHAPTERS 2–3

SUMMARY—CHAPTER 2: "SEARCH FOR MR. HYDE"

Utterson, prompted by his conversation with Enfield, goes home to study a will that he drew up for his close friend Dr. Jekyll. It states that in the event of the death or disappearance of Jekyll, all of his property should be given over immediately to a Mr. Edward Hyde. This strange will had long troubled Utterson, but now that he has heard something of Hyde's behavior, he becomes more upset and feels convinced that Hyde has some peculiar power over Jekyll. Seeking to unravel the mystery, he pays a visit to Dr. Lanyon, a friend of Jekyll's. But Lanyon has never heard of Hyde and has fallen out of communication with Jekyll as a result of a professional dispute. Lanyon refers to Jekyll's most recent line of research as "unscientific balderdash."

Later that night, Utterson is haunted by nightmares in which a faceless man runs down a small child and in which the same terrifying, faceless figure stands beside Jekyll's bed and commands him to rise. Soon, Utterson begins to spend time around the run-down building where Enfield saw Hyde enter, in the hopes of catching a glimpse of Hyde. Hyde, a small young man, finally appears, and Utterson approaches him. Utterson introduces himself as a friend of Henry Jekyll. Hyde, keeping his head down, returns his greetings. He asks Hyde to show him his face, so that he will know him if he sees him again; Hyde complies, and, like Enfield before him, Utterson feels appalled and horrified yet cannot pinpoint exactly what makes Hyde so ugly. Hyde then offers Utterson his address, which the lawyer interprets as a sign that Hyde eagerly anticipates the death of Jekyll and the execution of his will.

After this encounter, Utterson pays a visit to Jekyll. At this point, we learn what Utterson himself has known all along: namely, that the run-down building that Hyde frequents is actually a laboratory attached to Jekyll's well-kept townhouse, which faces outward on a parallel street. Utterson is admitted into Jekyll's home by Jekyll's butler, Mr. Poole, but Jekyll is not at home. Poole tells Utterson that Hyde has a key to the laboratory and that all the servants have orders to obey Hyde. The lawyer heads home, worrying about his friend. He assumes Hyde is blackmailing Jekyll, perhaps for some wrongdoings that Jekyll committed in his youth.

SUMMARY—CHAPTER 3: "DR. JEKYLL WAS QUITE AT EASE"

Two weeks later, Jekyll throws a well-attended dinner party. Utterson stays late so that the two men can speak privately. Utterson mentions the will, and Jekyll begins to make a joke about it, but he turns pale when Utterson tells him that he has been "learning something of young Hyde." Jekyll explains that the situation with Hyde is exceptional and cannot be solved by talking. He also insists that "the moment I choose, I can be rid of Mr. Hyde." But Jekyll emphasizes the great interest he currently takes in Hyde and his desire to continue to provide for him. He makes Utterson promise that he will carry out his will and testament.

ANALYSIS—CHAPTERS 2-3

Utterson behaves here like an amateur detective, as he does throughout the rest of the novel. However, unlike most detectives, he faces a gulf between what seems to be the factual evidence of the case and the supernatural reality behind it. This gulf is apparent in Utterson's reading of the will, for instance. On the face of it, Jekyll's stipulation that all his property be handed over to Hyde and his later horror at the thought of Utterson "learning something of young Hyde" seem to point squarely at blackmail of some sort. Of course, Utterson never imagines the situation that lies behind these behaviors. Similarly, the will's reference to "death or *disappearance*" (emphasis added) makes Utterson immediately think of the possibility of murder. The idea that Jekyll could literally transform himself into another and thereby disappear simply does not occur to Utterson, as it would not occur to any rational person. Utterson's failure to detect the truth does not demonstrate any failure in logic.

However, Stevenson does contrive to have his hardheaded lawyer access the dark supernatural undercurrents at work in the case of Jekyll and Hyde—if only in a limited way. Stevenson enlightens Utterson through the use of the dream sequence. In Utterson's dreams, the faceless figure of Hyde stalks through the city: "if at any time [Utterson] dozed over," the author writes, "it was but to see [Hyde] glide more stealthily through sleeping houses, or move the more swiftly . . . through wider labyrinths of lamplighted city, and at every street corner crush a child and leave her screaming." In Utterson's dreams, then, Hyde appears ubiquitous, permeating the city with his dark nature and his crimes. This idea of Hyde as a universal presence suggests that this faceless figure, crushing children and standing by Jekyll's bed, symbolizes all the secret sins that lurk beneath the surface of respectable London. This notion of hidden crimes recurs throughout the novel. It is significant that Stevenson never gives us any details of Jekyll's indiscretions prior to his creation of Hyde, nor of Hyde's wicked, dissipated habits. The crimes remain shrouded in mystery; to explain them in rational language would strip them of their supernatural and eerie quality.

Hyde's ugliness prompts a similar loss of words. When Utterson finally converses with Hyde and sees his face, like Enfield, he proves unable to comprehend and delineate exactly what makes Hyde so ugly and frightening. Significantly, though, one of the words that the fumbling lawyer comes up with is "troglodytic," a term referring to a prehistoric, manlike creature. Through this word, the text links the immoral Hyde to the notion of recidivism—a fall from civilization and a regression to a more primitive state. The imperialist age of Victorian England manifested a great fear of recidivism, particularly in its theories of racial science, in which theorists cautioned that lesser, savage peoples might swallow up the supposedly superior white races.

The description of Jekyll's house introduces an element of clear symbolism. The doctor lives in a well-appointed home, described by Stevenson as having "a great air of wealth and comfort." The building secretly connects to his laboratory, which faces out on another street and appears sinister and run-down. It is in the laboratory that Dr. Jekyll becomes Mr.

Hyde. Like the two secretly connected buildings, seemingly having nothing to do with each other but in fact easily traversed, the upstanding Jekyll and the corrupt Hyde appear separate but in fact share an unseen inner connection.

These chapters also introduce us to the minor character of Dr. Lanyon, Jekyll's former colleague. Lanyon's labeling of Jekyll's research as "unscientific balderdash" hints at the supernatural bent of the experiments, which contrasts powerfully with the prevailing scientific consensus of the Victorian world, in which rationalism and materialism held sway. In his reverence for the rational and logical, Lanyon emerges as the quintessential nineteenth-century scientist, automatically dismissing Jekyll's mystical experiments. Later events prove that his dogmatic faith in a purely material science is more akin to superstition than Jekyll's experiments.

CHAPTERS 4–5

SUMMARY—CHAPTER 4: "THE CAREW MURDER CASE"

Approximately one year later, the scene opens on a maid who, sitting at her window in the wee hours of the morning, witnesses a murder take place in the street below. She sees a small, evil-looking man, whom she recognizes as Mr. Hyde, encounter a polite, aged gentleman; when the gentleman offers Hyde a greeting, Hyde suddenly turns on him with a stick, beating him to death. The police find a letter addressed to Utterson on the dead body, and they consequently summon the lawyer. He identifies the body as Sir Danvers Carew, a popular member of Parliament and one of his clients.

Utterson still has Hyde's address, and he accompanies the police to a set of rooms located in a poor, evil-looking part of town. Utterson reflects on how odd it is that a man who lives in such squalor is the heir to Henry Jekyll's fortune. Hyde's villainous-looking landlady lets the men in, but the suspected murderer is not at home. The police find the murder weapon and the burned remains of Hyde's checkbook. Upon a subsequent visit to the bank, the police inspector learns that Hyde still has an account there. The officer assumes that he need only wait for Hyde to go and withdraw money. In the days and weeks that follow, however, no sign of Hyde turns up; he has no family, no friends, and those who have seen him are unable to give accurate descriptions, differ on details, and agree only on the evil aspect of his appearance.

SUMMARY—CHAPTER 5: "INCIDENT OF THE LETTER"

Utterson calls on Jekyll, whom he finds in his laboratory looking deathly ill. Jekyll feverishly claims that Hyde has left and that their relationship has ended. He also assures Utterson that the police shall never find the man. Jekyll then shows Utterson a letter and asks him what he should do with it, since he fears it could damage his reputation if he turns it over to the police. The letter is from Hyde, assuring Jekyll that he has means of escape, that Jekyll should not worry about him, and that he deems himself unworthy of Jekyll's great generosity. Utterson asks if Hyde dictated the terms of Jekyll's will—especially its insistence that Hyde inherit in the event of Jekyll's "disappearance." Jekyll replies in the affirmative, and Utterson tells his friend that Hyde probably meant to murder him and that he has had a near escape. He takes the letter and departs.

On his way out, Utterson runs into Poole, the butler, and asks him to describe the man who delivered the letter; Poole, taken aback, claims to have no knowledge of any letters being delivered other than the usual mail. That night, over drinks, Utterson consults his trusted clerk, Mr. Guest, who is an expert on handwriting. Guest compares Hyde's letter with some of Jekyll's own writing and suggests that the same hand inscribed both; Hyde's script merely leans in the opposite direction, as if for the purpose of concealment. Utterson reacts with alarm at the thought that Jekyll would forge a letter for a murderer.

ANALYSIS—CHAPTERS 4-5

Chapter 4 illustrates the extent of Hyde's capacity for evil. Whereas we might earlier take Hyde for nothing more than an unscrupulous opportunist, manipulating Jekyll, the mindlessly vicious nature of the man becomes clear with the violent murder of Sir Danvers Carew. Hyde is violent at random, with no apparent motive, and with little concern for his own safety—as his willingness to beat a man to death in the middle of a public street demonstrates. His complete disappearance after the murder, along with his utter lack of family, friends, and people who can identify him, suggests that he possesses some kind of otherworldly origin.

In Chapter 5, as in the rest of the novel, Utterson staunchly remains the proper Victorian gentleman, despite the disturbing nature of the events that he investigates. Even as he plays the detective, his principal desire remains the avoidance of scandal rather than the discovery of truth. Thus, even when he suspects Jekyll of covering up for a murderer, he reports nothing of it to anyone, preferring to set the matter aside in the hopes of preserving his client's reputation. Utterson's insistence on propriety and the maintenance of appearances deeply hinders his ability to learn the truth about Jekyll and Hyde. Moreover, this insistence reflects a shortcoming in the Victorian society that the lawyer represents. Stevenson suggests that society focuses so exclusively on outward appearances and respectability that it remains blind to the fact that human beings also possess a darker side, replete with malevolent instincts and irrational passions. Society, like Utterson, cannot see that a seemingly upstanding person can also possess an evil potential hidden within.

Yet, despite Utterson's straitlaced and unimaginative perspective on the mystery, the eerie aura of the situation reaches such intensity as to effect even this reserved gentleman. Earlier, Utterson has dreams in which London is transformed into a nightmare landscape through which Hyde stalks, committing violence against innocents. The image of the city as a place of hidden terrors recurs, but this time Utterson is awake and driving with the police to Hyde's rooms in the early morning. A fog has gripped London, and it swirls and eddies through the gloomy neighborhoods, making them seem "like a district of some city in a nightmare." As in all of his portrayals of London, Stevenson lavishes his descriptive skill on the passage, rendering the depicted landscape as a nest of hidden wickedness. Here, he describes the "great chocolate-coloured pall lowered over heaven . . . here it would be dark like the back-end of evening; and there would be a glow of a rich, lurid brown . . . and here . . . a haggard shaft of daylight would glance in between the swirling wreaths." It is important to note, however, that Stevenson attributes these poetic descriptions to Utterson. The words may seem out of character for the rather unimaginative lawyer, but one could also interpret them as testifying to the power of Hyde's horror. Perhaps the disturbing nature of Hyde's behavior and his residence bring out a darker side in Utterson himself, one in touch with the supernatural terrors lurking behind the facade of the everyday world.

The above passage offers an excellent example of Stevenson's ability to use evocative language to establish a sense of the uncanny in a narrative that is otherwise dry and forthright. Much of *Dr. Jekyll and Mr. Hyde* is written in a brisk, businesslike, and factual way, like a police report on a strange affair rather than a novel. This tone derives from the personality of Mr. Utterson but also seems to arise from the text itself. The original title, *The Strange Case of Dr. Jekyll and Mr. Hyde,* and chapter headings such as "Incident of the Letter" and "Incident at the Window" contribute to this reserved, dispassionate tone, as if detectives themselves have been titling each report for a ledger. But in passages like the one above, Stevenson injects rich, evocative descriptions into the narrative. This richer language performs a duty that Stevenson's placid characterization of Utterson does not; more important, it creates a link between the language of the text and the actions of the characters. The author thus not only hints at a darker side within Utterson but also at a darker side within the text itself, which typically keeps up appearances as a logical and linear narrative but periodically sinks into decadent flourishes. Utterson and the text, then, become metaphors for humanity in general, and for society at large, both of which may appear logically oriented and straightforward but, in fact, contain darker undercurrents.

CHAPTERS 6–7

SUMMARY—CHAPTER 6: "REMARKABLE INCIDENT OF DR. LANYON"

As time passes, with no sign of Hyde's reappearance, Jekyll becomes healthier-looking and more sociable, devoting himself to charity. To Utterson, it appears that the removal of Hyde's evil influence has had a tremendously positive effect on Jekyll. After two months of this placid lifestyle, Jekyll holds a dinner party, which both Utterson and Lanyon attend, and the three talk together as old friends. But a few days later, when Utterson calls on Jekyll, Poole reports that his master is receiving no visitors.

This scenario repeats itself for a week, so Utterson goes to visit Lanyon, hoping to learn why Jekyll has refused any company. He finds Lanyon in very poor health, pale and sickly, with a frightened look in his eyes. Lanyon explains that he has had a great shock and expects to die in a few weeks. "[L]ife has been pleasant," he says. "I liked it; yes, sir, I used to like it." Then he adds, "I sometimes think if we knew all, we should be more glad to get away." When Utterson mentions that Jekyll also seems ill, Lanyon violently demands that they talk of anything but Jekyll. He promises that after his death, Utterson may learn the truth about everything, but for now he will not discuss it. Afterward, at home, Utterson writes to Jekyll, talking about being turned away from Jekyll's house and inquiring as to what caused the break between him and Lanyon. Soon Jekyll's written reply arrives, explaining that while he still cares for Lanyon, he understands why the doctor says they must not meet. As for Jekyll himself, he pledges his continued affection for Utterson but adds that from now on he will be maintaining a strict seclusion, seeing no one. He says that he is suffering a punishment that he cannot name.

Lanyon dies a few weeks later, fulfilling his prophecy. After the funeral, Utterson takes from his safe a letter that Lanyon meant for him to read after he died. Inside, Utterson finds only another envelope, marked to remain sealed until

Jekyll also has died. Out of professional principle, Utterson overcomes his curiosity and puts the envelope away for safekeeping. As weeks pass, he calls on Jekyll less and less frequently, and the butler continues to refuse him entry.

SUMMARY—CHAPTER 7: "INCIDENT AT THE WINDOW"

The following Sunday, Utterson and Enfield are taking their regular stroll. Passing the door where Enfield once saw Hyde enter to retrieve Jekyll's check, Enfield remarks on the murder case. He notes that the story that began with the trampling has reached an end, as London will never again see Mr. Hyde. Enfield mentions that in the intervening weeks he has learned that the run-down laboratory they pass is physically connected to Jekyll's house, and they both stop to peer into the house's windows, with Utterson noting his concern for Jekyll's health. To their surprise, the two men find Jekyll at the window, enjoying the fresh air. Jekyll complains that he feels "very low," and Utterson suggests that he join them for a walk, to help his circulation. Jekyll refuses, saying that he cannot go out. Then, just as they resume polite conversation, a look of terror seizes his face, and he quickly shuts the window and vanishes. Utterson and Enfield depart in shocked silence.

ANALYSIS—CHAPTERS 6-7

By this point in the story, it becomes clear that the mystery of Jekyll's relationship to Hyde has proven too much for Utterson's rational approach and search for logical explanations. The uncanny aspects of Hyde's appearance, behavior, and ability to disappear should suffice to indicate the fantastical air of the situation. At this point, however, the strange tragedy surrounding Lanyon roots the mystery in distinctly supernatural territory. Until this point, Lanyon's main significance to the story has been his function as a representative of reason. He dismisses Jekyll's experiments as "unscientific balderdash" and embodies the rational man of science, in distinct opposition to superstition and fantasy. Ironically, all of Lanyon's earlier sentiments seem to have given way to a cryptic, unexplained horror. Lanyon's deterioration mirrors the gradual erosion of logic in the face of the supernatural in the novel.

This erosion is accompanied by a further breakdown of language. As we see earlier, *Dr. Jekyll and Mr. Hyde* seems to present language—a rational, logical mode of perceiving and containing the world—as existing in opposition to the fanciful or fantastical. For example, Stevenson refrains from describing Hyde's crimes or Jekyll's youthful debaucheries in detail, as if such explanations might reduce the haunting effect of these wicked actions. Correspondingly, just as language might break down and defuse an aura of the uncanny, the uncanny can prompt a breakdown in language. Hyde's ugliness instigates one such loss of words. As we have seen, when Enfield and Utterson see Hyde's face, they prove unable to describe what exactly makes Hyde so ugly and frightening.

But the novel is permeated by other silences as well, more akin to refusals than failures to speak: Lanyon refuses to describe to Utterson what he has seen; Jekyll declines to discuss his relationship with Hyde; after witnessing Jekyll's strange disappearance from the window, Utterson and Enfield say almost nothing about it; and Utterson carries out an informal investigation of Hyde and Jekyll but never mentions his suspicions to anyone. This second set of silences derives not so much from being involuntarily awestruck by the uncanny, but rather points to an acknowledgment of a situation that exceeds the boundaries of logic, yet with an unwillingness to pursue it further or express it openly. Such unwillingness seems to stem, in turn, from a concern for reputation and public morality. Significantly, both Jekyll and Lanyon leave written records of what they have seen and done but insist that these records not be opened until after their deaths. In other words, the truth can be exposed only after the death of the person whose reputation it might ruin. Stevenson may suggest that such refusals to discuss the grittier side of life mirror a similar tendency in Victorian society at large.

CHAPTER 8: "THE LAST NIGHT"

SUMMARY

Jekyll's butler Poole visits Utterson one night after dinner. Deeply agitated, he says only that he believes there has been some "foul play" regarding Dr. Jekyll; he quickly brings Utterson to his master's residence. The night is dark and windy, and the streets are deserted, giving Utterson a premonition of disaster. When he reaches Jekyll's house, he finds the servants gathered fearfully in the main hall. Poole brings Utterson to the door of Jekyll's laboratory and calls inside, saying that Utterson has come for a visit. A strange voice responds, sounding nothing like that of Jekyll; the owner of the voice tells Poole that he can receive no visitors.

Poole and Utterson retreat to the kitchen, where Poole insists that the voice they heard emanating from the laboratory does not belong to his master. Utterson wonders why the murderer would remain in the laboratory if he had just killed Jekyll and not simply flee. Poole describes how the mystery voice has sent him on constant errands to chemists; the man in the laboratory seems desperate for some ingredient that no drugstore in London sells. Utterson, still hopeful, asks whether the notes Poole has received are in the doctor's hand, but Poole then reveals that he has seen the person inside the laboratory, when he came out briefly to search for something, and that the man looked nothing like Jekyll. Utterson suggests that Jekyll may have some disease that changes his voice and deforms his features, making them unrecognizable, but Poole declares that the person he saw was smaller than his master—and looked, in fact, like none other than Mr. Hyde.

Hearing Poole's words, Utterson resolves that he and Poole should break into the laboratory. He sends two servants around the block to the laboratory's other door, the one that Enfield sees Hyde using at the beginning of the novel. Then, armed with a fireplace poker and an axe, Utterson and Poole return to the inner door. Utterson calls inside, demanding admittance. The voice begs for Utterson to have mercy and to leave him alone. The lawyer, however, recognizes the voice as Hyde's and orders Poole to smash down the door.

Once inside, the men find Hyde's body lying on the floor, a crushed vial in his hand. He appears to have poisoned himself. Utterson notes that Hyde is wearing a suit that belongs to Jekyll and that is much too large for him. The men search the entire laboratory, as well as the surgeon's theater below and the other rooms in the building, but they find neither a trace of Jekyll nor a corpse. They note a large mirror and think it strange to find such an item in a scientific laboratory. Then, on Jekyll's business table, they find a large envelope addressed to Utterson that contains three items. The first is a will, much like the previous one, except that it replaces

Hyde's name with Utterson's. The second is a note to Utterson, with the present day's date on it. Based on this piece of evidence, Utterson surmises that Jekyll is still alive—and he wonders if Hyde really died by suicide or if Jekyll killed him. This note instructs Utterson to go home immediately and read the letter that Lanyon gave him earlier. It adds that if he desires to learn more, Utterson can read the confession of "Your worthy and unhappy friend, Henry Jekyll." Utterson takes the third item from the envelope—a sealed packet—and promises Poole that he will return that night and send for the police. He then heads back to his office to read Lanyon's letter and the contents of the sealed packet.

ANALYSIS

In the classic detective story, this climactic chapter would contain the scene in which the detective, having solved the case, reveals his ingenious solution and fingers the culprit. But, in spite of Utterson's efforts in investigating the matter of Jekyll and Hyde, he has made no progress in solving the mystery. Indeed, were it not for the existence of Lanyon's letter and Jekyll's confession, which make up the last two chapters, it seems likely that the truth about Jekyll and Hyde never would be ascertained.

One cannot blame Utterson for failing to solve the case of Jekyll and Hyde before reading the letters—even the most skilled professional detective could not have deduced the supernatural circumstances surrounding the doctor and his darker half. Nevertheless, Stevenson uses this chapter to emphasize just how far away from the truth Utterson remains, extending almost to the point of absurdity. The servants, led by Poole, remain more in touch with the reality of the situation; they *know* that something terrible has happened to their master, and so they forsake their duties and huddle together out of fright. Upon seeing them gathered in fear, Utterson reacts with a response characteristic of his all-consuming concern for propriety and the upkeep of appearances. Instead of looking for the cause of the servants' terror, he is more concerned with maintaining decorum and social hierarchy. "What, what?" he bursts out. "Are you all here? . . . Very irregular, very unseemly; your master would be far from pleased."

Even at this time of clear crisis, Utterson is unwilling to allow for any breach of propriety and order. As he talks with Poole before the locked door of the laboratory, Utterson is growing desperate to avoid taking action. He offers more and more absurd explanations for what Poole has seen that culminate in his suggestion that Jekyll has a disease that has changed his appearance to the point of unrecognizability. Utterson is willing to accept any explanation, however improbable, before doing anything so indecorous as breaking down a door. Moreover, his unwillingness to break into Jekyll's laboratory reflects his continued concern for his friend's reputation. As long as he does not break in, he seems to think, Jekyll's good name will be preserved. In portraying Utterson's absurd mindset, Stevenson seems to comment on the larger Victorian mentality and on what one might see as its privileging of order and decorum over truth.

But Utterson's unwillingness to penetrate the mystery of his friend's situation is more than the expression of his Victorian desire to avoid scandal. He seems to have a premonition that what awaits him in the laboratory constitutes not merely a breach of order but the toppling of one order by another. His conversation with Poole is a frantic attempt to avoid entering the world of supernatural terrors that Jekyll has loosed.

It is this sense of supernatural terror breaking into everyday reality that places *Dr. Jekyll and Mr. Hyde* firmly within the tradition of Gothic fiction, which flourished in nineteenth-century Europe—and particularly in Britain, where such Gothic masterpieces as *Dracula, The Turn of the Screw, Frankenstein,* and *Jane Eyre* were penned. The term "Gothic" covers a wide variety of stories, but certain recurring themes and motifs define the genre. Gothic tales may contain explicitly supernatural material, as *Dracula* does, or imply supernatural phenomena without narrating it directly, as *Jekyll and Hyde* does. They may not allude to supernatural events at all, but simply convey a sense of the uncanny, of dark and disturbing elements that break into the routine of prosaic, everyday life, as *Jane Eyre* does. Gothic novels often center around secrets—such as Jekyll's connection to Hyde—or around doppelgängers, a German term referring to people who resemble other characters in strange, disconcerting ways. Frankenstein's monster is a doppelgänger for Frankenstein, just as Hyde is for Jekyll. Above all, Gothic novels depend upon geography for their power. Nearly every Gothic novel takes place in some strange, eerie locale from which the characters have difficulty escaping, be it Dracula's castle, the estate of Thornfield in *Jane Eyre,* or the decaying homes and palaces that appear in the stories of the greatest practitioner of American Gothic fiction, Edgar Allan Poe. In *Dr. Jekyll and Mr. Hyde,* of course, that uncanny place is the fog-blanketed world of nighttime London.

Although the dialogue in this chapter arguably interrupts the dramatic momentum of the situation, Stevenson nevertheless conjures a mood of dread, primarily through the use of evocative language. For example, as Poole and Utterson stand ready to break down the door, the text declares that "[t]he scud had banked over the moon, and it was now quite dark. The wind, which only broke in puffs and draughts into that deep well of building, tossed the light of the candle to and fro about their steps." And earlier, as Utterson and Poole travel through the empty streets to reach Jekyll's home, Stevenson revisits his frequent image of London as a nightmare city, where darkness—both moral and physical—holds sway.

CHAPTER 9: "DR. LANYON'S NARRATIVE"

SUMMARY

> *He put the glass to his lips, and drank at one gulp. . . . there before my eyes . . . there stood Henry Jekyll!*
>
> (See Quotations, p. 151)

This chapter constitutes a word-for-word transcription of the letter Lanyon intends Utterson to open after Lanyon and Jekyll's deaths. Lanyon writes that after Jekyll's last dinner party, he received a strange letter from Jekyll. The letter asked Lanyon to go to Jekyll's home and, with the help of Poole, break into the upper room—or "cabinet"—of Jekyll's laboratory. The letter instructed Lanyon then to remove a specific drawer and all its contents from the laboratory, return with this drawer to his own home, and wait for a man who would come to claim it precisely at midnight. The letter seemed to Lanyon to have been written in a mood of desperation. It offered no explanation for the orders it gave but promised Lanyon that if he did as it bade, he would soon understand everything.

Lanyon duly went to Jekyll's home, where Poole and a locksmith met him. The locksmith broke into the lab, and Lanyon returned home with the drawer. Within the drawer, Lanyon found several vials, one containing what seemed to be salt and another holding a peculiar red liquid. The drawer also contained a notebook recording what seemed to be years of experiments, with little notations such as "double" or "total failure!!!" scattered amid a long list of dates. However, the notebooks offered no hints as to what the experiments involved. Lanyon waited for his visitor, increasingly certain that Jekyll must be insane. As promised, at the stroke of midnight, a small, evil-looking man appeared, dressed in clothes much too large for him. It was, of course, Mr. Hyde, but Lanyon, never having seen the man before, did not recognize him. Hyde seemed nervous and excited. He avoided polite conversation, interested only in the contents of the drawer. Lanyon directed him to it, and Hyde then asked for a graduated glass. In it, he mixed the ingredients from the drawer to form a purple liquid, which then became green. Hyde paused and asked Lanyon whether he should leave and take the glass with him, or whether he should stay and drink it in front of Lanyon, allowing the doctor to witness something that he claimed would "stagger the unbelief of Satan." Lanyon, irritated, declared that he had already become so involved in the matter that he wanted to see the end of it.

Taking up the glass, Hyde told Lanyon that his skepticism of "transcendental medicine" would now be disproved. Before Lanyon's eyes, the deformed man drank the glass in one gulp and then seemed to swell, his body expanding, his face melting and shifting, until, shockingly, Hyde was gone and Dr. Jekyll stood in his place. Lanyon here ends his letter, stating that what Jekyll told him afterward is too shocking to repeat and that the horror of the event has so wrecked his constitution that he will soon die.

ANALYSIS

This chapter finally makes explicit the nature of Dr. Jekyll's relationship to his darker half, Mr. Hyde—the men are one and the same person. Lanyon's narrative offers a smaller mystery within the larger mystery of the novel: the doctor is presented with a puzzling set of instructions from his friend Jekyll without any explanation of what the instructions mean. We know more than Lanyon, of course, and instantly realize that the small man who strikes Lanyon with a "disgustful curiosity" can be none other than Hyde. But even this knowledge does not diminish the shocking effect of the climax of the novel, the moment when we finally witness the interchange between the two identities. Through the astonished eyes of Lanyon, Stevenson offers a vivid description, using detailed language and imagery to lend immediacy to supernatural events.

Yet it is worth noting that for all the details that the doctor's account includes, this chapter offers very little *explanation* of what Lanyon sees. We learn that Hyde and Jekyll are the same person and that the two personas can morph into one another with the help of a mysterious potion. We remain largely in the dark, however, as to how or why this situation came about. Lanyon states that Jekyll told him everything after the transformation was complete, but he refrains from telling Utterson, declaring that "[w]hat he told me in the next hour I cannot bring my mind to set on paper."

As with previous silences in the novel, this silence owes to a character's refusal to confront truths that upset his worldview. As we have seen in previous chapters, Jekyll has delved into mystical investigations of the nature of man, whereas Lanyon has adhered strictly to rational, materialist science. Indeed, in some sense, Lanyon cannot conceive of the world that Jekyll has entered; thus, when he is forced to confront this world as manifested in Hyde's transformation, he retreats deep within himself, spurning this phenomenon that shatters his worldview. The impact of the shock is such that it causes Lanyon, a scientist committed to pursuing knowledge, to declare in Chapter 6, "I sometimes think if we knew all, we should be more glad to get away." Lanyon has decided that some knowledge is not worth the cost of obtaining or possessing it. Like Utterson and Enfield, he prefers silence to the exposure of dark truths. The task of exposing these truths must fall to Henry Jekyll himself, in the final chapter of the novel. As the only character to have embraced the darker side of the world, Jekyll remains the only one willing to speak of it.

CHAPTER 10: "HENRY JEKYLL'S FULL STATEMENT OF THE CASE"

SUMMARY

> *I learned to recognise the thorough and primitive duality of man . . . if I could rightly be said to be either, it was only because I was radically both.*
>
> (See Quotations, p. 153)

This chapter offers a transcription of the letter Jekyll leaves for Utterson in the laboratory. Jekyll writes that upon his birth he possessed a large inheritance, a healthy body, and a hardworking, decent nature. His idealism allowed him to maintain a respectable seriousness in public while hiding his more frivolous and indecent side. By the time he was fully grown, he found himself leading a dual life, in which his better side constantly felt guilt for the transgressions of his darker side. When his scientific interests led to mystical studies as to the divided nature of man, he hoped to find some solution to his own split nature. Jekyll insists that "man is not truly one, but truly two," and he records how he dreamed of separating the good and evil natures.

Jekyll reports that, after much research, he eventually found a chemical solution that might serve his purposes. Buying a large quantity of salt as his last ingredient, he took the potion with the knowledge that he was risking his life, but he remained driven by the hopes of making a great discovery. At first, he experienced incredible pain and nausea. But as these symptoms subsided, he felt vigorous and filled with recklessness and sensuality. He had become the shrunken, deformed Mr. Hyde. He hypothesizes that Hyde's small stature owed to the fact that this persona represented his evil side alone, which up to that point had been repressed.

Upon first looking into a mirror after the transformation, Jekyll-turned-Hyde was not repulsed by his new form; instead, he experienced "a leap of welcome." He came to delight in living as Hyde. Jekyll was becoming too old to act upon his more embarrassing impulses, but Hyde was a younger man, the personification of the evil side that emerged several years after Jekyll's own birth. Transforming himself into Hyde became a welcome outlet for Jekyll's passions. Jekyll furnished a home and set up a bank account for his alter ego, Hyde, who soon sunk into utter degradation. But each time he transformed back into Jekyll, he felt no guilt at Hyde's dark exploits, though he did try to right whatever wrongs had been done.

It was not until two months before the Carew murder that Jekyll found cause for concern. While asleep one night, he involuntarily transformed into Hyde—without the help of the potion—and awoke in the body of his darker half. This incident convinced him that he must cease with his transformations or risk being trapped in Hyde's form forever. But after two months as Jekyll, he caved in and took the potion again. Hyde, so long repressed, emerged wild and vengefully savage, and it was in this mood that he beat Carew to death, delighting in the crime. Hyde showed no remorse for the murder, but Jekyll knelt and prayed to God for forgiveness even before his transformation back was complete. The horrifying nature of the murder convinced Jekyll never to transform himself again, and it was during the subsequent months that Utterson and others remarked that Jekyll seemed to have had a weight lifted from his shoulders, and that everything seemed well with him.

Eventually, though, Jekyll grew weary of constant virtue and indulged some of his darker desires—in his own person, not that of Hyde. But this dip into darkness proved sufficient to cause another spontaneous transformation into Hyde, which took place one day when Jekyll was sitting in a park, far from home. As Hyde, he immediately felt brave and powerful, but he also knew that the police would seize him for his murder of Carew. He could not even return to his rooms to get his potions without a great risk of being captured. It was then that he sent word to Lanyon to break into his laboratory and get his potions for him. After that night, he had to take a double dose of the potion every six hours to avoid spontaneous transformations into Hyde. As soon as the drug began to wear off, the transformation process would begin. It was one of these spells that struck him as he spoke to Enfield and Utterson out the window, forcing him to withdraw.

In his last, desperate hours, Hyde grew stronger as Jekyll grew weaker. Moreover, the salt necessary for the potion began to run out. Jekyll ordered more, only to discover that the mineral did not have the same effect; he realized that the original salt must have contained an impurity that made the potion work. Jekyll then anticipated the fast approach of the moment when he must become Hyde permanently. He thus used the last of the potion to buy himself time during which to compose this final letter. Jekyll writes that he does not know whether, when faced with discovery, Hyde will kill himself or be arrested and hanged—but he knows that by the time Utterson reads this letter, Henry Jekyll will be no more.

> *[As] the first edge of my penitence wore off . . . a qualm came over me, a horrid nausea and the most deadly shuddering.*
>
> (See Quotations, p. 154)

ANALYSIS

At this point all the mysteries of the novel unravel, as we encounter a second account of the same events that have been unfolding throughout the novel. Only this time, instead of seeing them from the point of view of Utterson, we see them from the point of view of Jekyll—and, by extension, that of Hyde. This shift in point of view makes a great difference indeed. All the events that seemed puzzling or inexplicable before are suddenly explained: Jekyll's confession makes clear the will that left everything to Hyde; it tells of the events leading up to the brutal murder of Carew; it clarifies the mystery of the similarity between Jekyll and Hyde's handwritings; it elucidates why Jekyll seemed to improve dramatically after Carew's murder, and why he abruptly went into a decline and was forced into seclusion. We know, finally, the details behind Hyde's midnight visit to Lanyon and Jekyll's bizarre disappearance from the window while talking to Enfield and Utterson; so, too, is Jekyll's final disappearance explained. It is as if there have been two parallel narratives throughout the novel, and we have, until now, been given access only to one. With Jekyll's confession, however, everything falls into place.

Jekyll's meditations on the dual nature of man, which prompt his forays into the experiments that bring forth Hyde, point to the novel's central question about the nature of the relationship between the good and evil portions of the human soul. As the embodiment of the dark side of man, Hyde is driven by passion and heedless of moral constraints. Yet it is important to note that while Hyde exists as distilled evil, Jekyll remains a mixture of good and evil. Jekyll repeatedly claims that his goal was to liberate his light half from his darker impulses, yet the opposite seems to happen. His dark side is given flesh, while his better half is not. Moreover, his dark side grows ever stronger as the novel continues, until the old, half-good and half-evil Jekyll ceases to exist.

Hyde is smaller than Jekyll, and younger, which leads Jekyll to surmise that his evil part is smaller and less developed than his good part. Yet Hyde's physical strength might suggest the opposite—that the evil side possesses a superior power and vigor. Jekyll's initial delight whenever he becomes Hyde seems to support this viewpoint, as does the fact that, no matter how appalling the crimes Hyde commits, Jekyll never feels guilty enough to refrain from making the transformation again as soon as he feels the urge. "Henry Jekyll stood at times aghast before the acts of Edward Hyde," Jekyll writes, "but the situation was apart from ordinary laws, and insidiously relaxed the grasp of conscience. It was Hyde, after all, and Hyde alone, that was guilty." But such statements seem little more than an absurd attempt at self-justification. For it is Jekyll who brings Hyde into being, clearly knowing that he embodies pure evil. Jekyll therefore bears responsibility for Hyde's actions. Indeed, his willingness to convince himself otherwise suggests, again, that the darker half of the man has the upper hand, even when he is Jekyll and not Hyde.

With these pieces of evidence, Stevenson suggests the immensity of humanity's dark impulses, which conscience can barely hold in check. In the end, then, although he portrays Utterson and Enfield as somewhat absurd in their denial of evil, Stevenson also may sympathize with their determination to repress their dark sides completely. Evil may be so strong that such strategies offer the only possibility for order and morality in society. The alternative—actively exploring the darkness—leads one into the trap that closes permanently on the hapless Jekyll, whose conscientious, civilized self proves no match for the violence unleashed in the person of Hyde.

Interestingly, even in this confessional chapter, certain details of the story's horrors remain obscure. Jekyll refuses to give any description of his youthful sins, and he does not actually elaborate on any of the "depravity"—except the murder of Carew—in which Hyde engages. As with other silences in the book, this absence of explanation may point to the clash between rational articulation and the irrationality of profound evil. Perhaps these deeds are so depraved that they defy all attempts at true explanation, or perhaps

Stevenson fears that to describe them explicitly would be to destroy their eerie power.

But in this chapter in particular, the silence may also indicate not a failure of words but, as in other instances, a refusal to use them. Earlier in the novel, reserved and decorous men such as Enfield and Utterson, wanting to deny the darker elements of humanity, make such a refusal. Here, however, one can hardly ascribe the silences to a character's denial of evil, since the letter that constitutes this chapter comes from Jekyll himself. The absence of description may owe not to any repression within the novel itself but to the repressive tendencies of the world in which Stevenson wrote. Rigid Victorian norms would not have allowed him to elaborate upon Jekyll and Hyde's crimes if they were tremendously gruesome; Stevenson thus discusses them in a vague (and thus acceptable) manner.

While Victorian society forbade the discussion of many issues, sexuality stood at the top of the blacklist. Based on other indications in the novel, one can reasonably infer that the misdeeds of Jekyll and Hyde are sexual in nature. For example, upon the novel's introduction of Hyde, Hyde tramples a young girl underfoot and then pays off her family. Child prostitution was rampant in Victorian London, and there may be a suggestion of it here. Moreover, in a novel whose characters are all staunch bachelors, one might interpret the "depravity" mentioned in the text as acts of hidden homosexuality. Late Victorian literature contains many subtle allusions to covert acts of socially unaccepted sexual behavior, often referring to or symbolizing homosexual activities. Oscar Wilde's novel *The Picture of Dorian Gray* provides an excellent example of Victorian literature's concern and anxiety regarding sexual orientation.

In the end, though, the actual nature of Hyde and Jekyll's sins proves less important than Stevenson's larger point, which is that the lure of the dark side constitutes a universal part of our human nature. We are all Jekylls, desperately trying to keep our Hydes under control—even as we are secretly fascinated by what they do and envious of their frightening freedom from moral constraints.

Important Quotations Explained

1. *Mr. Utterson the lawyer was a man of a rugged countenance, that was never lighted by a smile; cold, scanty and embarrassed in discourse; backward in sentiment; lean, long, dusty, dreary, and yet somehow lovable. . . . He was austere with himself; drank gin when he was alone, to mortify a taste for vintages; and though he enjoyed the theatre, had not crossed the doors of one for twenty years. But he had an approved tolerance for others; sometimes wondering, almost with envy, at the high pressure of spirits involved in their misdeeds; and in any extremity inclined to help rather than to reprove. . . . [I]t was frequently his fortune to be the last reputable acquaintance and the last good influence in the lives of down-going men.*

This passage is taken from the first paragraph of the novel, in which Stevenson sketches the character of Utterson the lawyer, through whose eyes the bulk of the novel unfolds. In a sense, Utterson comes across as an uninteresting character—unsmiling, "scanty" in speech, "lean, long, dusty, dreary" in person. As we know from later passages in the novel, he never stoops to gossip and struggles to maintain propriety even to the point of absurdity; the above passage notes the man's "auster[ity]."

Yet this introductory passage also reveals certain cracks

in this rigid, civilized facade—cracks that make Utterson an ideal person to pursue the bizarre case of Jekyll and Hyde. For one thing, the passage draws attention to Utterson's "lovab[ility]," his tendency to "help rather than to reprove." This geniality and approachability positions Utterson at the center of the novel's social web—all of the other characters confide in him and turn to him for help, allowing him glimpses of the mystery from every point of view. Both Lanyon and Jekyll confide in him; his friendship with Enfield gives him a salient piece of information early in the novel; Poole comes to him when Jekyll's situation reaches a crisis point. Utterson even serves as the attorney for Sir Danvers Carew, Hyde's victim. Second, the passage notes Utterson's keen interest in individuals with dark secrets, in those who suffer from scandal. Indeed, the text observes, Utterson sometimes wonders with near "envy" at the motivations behind people's wrongdoings or missteps. It is this curiosity, seemingly out of place in a dully respectable man, that prompts him to involve himself in the unfolding mystery.

2. *"He is not easy to describe. There is something wrong with his appearance; something displeasing, something downright detestable. I never saw a man I so disliked, and yet I scarce know why. He must be deformed somewhere; he gives a strong feeling of deformity, although I couldn't specify the point. He's an extraordinary-looking man, and yet I really can name nothing out of the way. No, sir; I can make no hand of it; I can't describe him. And it's not want of memory; for I declare I can see him this moment."*

This quotation appears in Chapter 1, "Story of the Door," when Enfield relates to Utterson how he watched Hyde trample a little girl underfoot. Utterson asks his friend to describe Hyde's appearance, but Enfield, as the quote indicates, proves unable to formulate a clear portrait. He asserts that Hyde is deformed, ugly, and inspires an immediate revulsion, yet he cannot say why.

Enfield's lack of eloquence sets a pattern for the novel, as no one—from Utterson himself to witnesses describing Hyde to the police—can come up with an exact description of the man. Most people merely conclude that he appears ugly and deformed in some indefinable way. These failures of articulation create an impression of Hyde as an uncanny figure, someone whose deformity is truly intangible, mysterious, perceptible only with some sort of sixth sense for which no vocabulary exists. It is almost as if language itself fails when it tries to come to grips with Hyde; he is beyond words, just as he is beyond morality and conscience. As a supernatural creation, he does not quite belong in the world; correspondingly, he evades the conceptual faculties of normal human beings.

3. *He put the glass to his lips, and drank at one gulp. A cry followed; he reeled, staggered, clutched at the table and held on, staring with injected eyes, gasping with open mouth; and as I looked there came, I thought, a change—he seemed to swell—his face became suddenly black and the features seemed to melt and alter—and at the next moment, I had sprung to my feet and leaped back against the wall, my arm raised to*

> *shield me from that prodigy, my mind submerged in terror.*
>
> *"O God!" I screamed, and "O God!" again and again; for there before my eyes—pale and shaken, and half fainting, and groping before him with his hands, like a man restored from death—there stood Henry Jekyll!*

This quotation appears in Chapter 9, "Dr. Lanyon's Narrative," as Lanyon describes the moment when Hyde, drinking the potion whose ingredients Lanyon procured from Jekyll's laboratory, transforms himself back into Jekyll. Lanyon, who earlier ridicules Jekyll's experiments as "unscientific balderdash," now sees the proof of Jekyll's success. The sight so horrifies him that he dies shortly after this scene. The transformation constitutes the climactic moment in the story, when all the questions about Jekyll's relationship to Hyde suddenly come to a resolution.

Stevenson heightens the effect of his climax by describing the scene in intensely vivid language. When he depicts Hyde as "staring with injected eyes" and suggests the dreadful contortions of his features as they "melt and alter," he superbly evokes the ghastliness of the moment of transformation. As this passage emphasizes, the true horror of Jekyll and Hyde's secret is not that they are two sides of the same person, each persona able to assert itself at will, but that each is actually trapped within the grip of the other, fighting for dominance. The transformation process appears fittingly violent and ravaging, causing the metamorphosing body to "reel," "stagger," and "gasp." Indeed, by this point in the novel, Jekyll is losing ground to Hyde, and, correspondingly, emerges "half fainting," as if "restored from death."

> 4. *It was on the moral side, and in my own person, that I learned to recognise the thorough and primitive duality of man; I saw that, of the two natures that contended in the field of my consciousness, even if I could rightly be said to be either, it was only because I was radically both; and from an early date . . . I had learned to dwell with pleasure, as a beloved daydream, on the thought of the separation of these elements.*

This quotation appears midway through Chapter 10, "Henry Jekyll's Full Statement of the Case," which consists of the letter that Jekyll leaves for Utterson. The letter allows us finally to glimpse the events of the novel from the inside. In this passage, Jekyll discusses the years leading up to his discovery of the potion that transforms him into Hyde. He summarizes his theory of humanity's dual nature, which states that human beings are half virtuous and half criminal, half moral and half amoral. Jekyll's goal in his experiments is to separate these two elements, creating a being of pure good and a being of pure evil. In this way he seeks to free his good side from dark urges while liberating his wicked side from the pangs of conscience. Ultimately, however, Jekyll succeeds only in separating out Hyde, his evil half, while he himself remains a mix of good and evil. And eventually, of course, Hyde begins to predominate, until Jekyll ceases to exist and only Hyde remains. This outcome suggests a possible fallacy in Jekyll's original assumptions. Perhaps he did not possess an equally balanced good half and evil half, as he thought. The events of the novel imply that the dark side (Hyde) is far stronger than the rest of Jekyll—so strong that, once sent free, this side takes him over completely.

5. *[B]ut I was still cursed with my duality of purpose; and as the first edge of my penitence wore off, the lower side of me, so long indulged, so recently chained down, began to growl for licence. Not that I dreamed of resuscitating Hyde; . . . no, it was in my own person that I was once more tempted to trifle with my conscience. . . .*

   [However,] this brief condescension to my evil finally destroyed the balance of my soul. And yet I was not alarmed; the fall seemed natural, like a return to the old days before I had made discovery. It was a fine . . . day . . . I sat in the sun on a bench; the animal within me licking the chops of memory; the spiritual side a little drowsed, promising subsequent penitence, but not yet moved to begin. After all, I reflected, I was like my neighbours; and then I smiled, comparing myself with other men, comparing my active goodwill with the lazy cruelty of their neglect. And at the very moment of that vainglorious thought, a qualm came over me, a horrid nausea and the most deadly shuddering. . . . I began to be aware of a

> *change in the temper of my thoughts, a greater boldness, a contempt of danger, a solution of the bonds of obligation. I looked down; my clothes hung formlessly on my shrunken limbs; the hand that lay on my knee was corded and hairy. I was once more Edward Hyde.*

These words appear in Jekyll's confession, near the end of Chapter 10, and they mark the point at which Hyde finally and inalterably begins to dominate the Jekyll-Hyde relationship; Jekyll begins to transform into his darker self spontaneously, without the aid of his potion, and while wide awake. In the particular instance described in the passage, it only takes a single prideful thought to effect the transformation—although that thought comes on the heels of a Jekyll's dip into his old, pre-Hyde debauchery. As elsewhere, the novel gives no details here of the exact sins involved in Jekyll's "brief condescension to evil," and thus when he mentions "the animal within me licking the chops of memory," we are left to imagine what dark deeds Jekyll remembers. Again, the language of this passage emphasizes Jekyll's dualistic theory of human nature, as he contrasts "the animal within me" to his "spiritual side." And the text deliberately presents Hyde's body as animal-like, especially in the reference to a "corded and hairy" hand. In addition, Stevenson describes Jekyll's longing as a "growl for licence," which, ironically, is reminiscent of animals communicating with each other. In a novel intentionally devoid of billowy language and concerned more with providing a record than with developing verbal description, Jekyll can be most vocally expressive of his desires when he longs to transform into

Hyde. As Hyde, he loses the conscious abilities to form language completely, falling victim to the instincts within and losing the ability to recall exactly what is happening. The above description implies that Jekyll, in becoming Hyde, is regressing into the primitive and coming closer to the violent, amoral world of animals.

Key Facts

FULL TITLE

The Strange Case of Dr. Jekyll and Mr. Hyde

AUTHOR

Robert Louis Stevenson

TYPE OF WORK

Novel

GENRE

Gothic mystery story

LANGUAGE

English

TIME AND PLACE WRITTEN

1885, Bournemouth, England

DATE OF FIRST PUBLICATION

January 1886

PUBLISHER

Longmans, Green and Co.

NARRATOR

The narrator is anonymous and speaks in the third person. Dr. Lanyon and Dr. Jekyll each narrate one chapter of the novel via a confessional letter.

POINT OF VIEW

For most of the novel, the narrative follows Utterson's point of view; in the last two chapters, Lanyon and Jekyll report their experiences from their own perspectives.

TONE

Mysterious; serious

TENSE

Past

SETTING (TIME)

The late nineteenth century

SETTING (PLACE)

London

PROTAGONIST

Henry Jekyll

MAJOR CONFLICT

Jekyll attempts to keep his dark half, Edward Hyde, under control and then to prevent himself from becoming Hyde permanently.

RISING ACTION

Utterson attempts to discover the truth about the Jekyll-Hyde relationship.

CLIMAX

One could argue for two different climaxes. The moment when Utterson breaks down the door to Jekyll's laboratory and finds Hyde's corpse constitutes a climax in that Utterson finally admits and accepts that something terribly wrong has taken place. But one might also see the novel's climax as arising within Lanyon's letter, at the moment that he witnesses Hyde's transformation into Jekyll and the mysterious connection between the personas is finally explained.

FALLING ACTION

Utterson leaves Jekyll's laboratory, goes home, and reads the letters from Lanyon and Jekyll, which explain all.

THEMES

The duality of human nature; the importance of reputation

MOTIFS

Violence against innocents; silence; urban terror

SYMBOLS

Jekyll's house and laboratory; Hyde's physical appearance

FORESHADOWING

While a general mood of impending disaster pervades the novel, there are few instances of explicit foreshadowing.

Reading Group Questions

1. Analyze the different stages of Jekyll's experimentation with the Hyde persona. How do his feelings regarding the transformations change?

2. How does Jekyll interpret his relationship to Hyde? Do you agree with his understanding? Why or why not?

3. Examine the role of the minor characters in the novel, including Lanyon, Enfield, Carew, and Poole. How does Utterson's connection to each of these men serve to advance the plot?

4. At one point in the novel, Hyde is described as "troglodytic." To what does this term refer? What was its significance in Victorian England? How does it relate to the themes of the novel?

5. Why do you think Stevenson chose to tell the story from Utterson's point of view rather than use Jekyll's from the beginning? How does this choice increase the suspense of the novel?

Study Questions

1. *How does Utterson perceive the relationship between Jekyll and Hyde for most of the novel? Is his interpretation understandable? What are the limits of his knowledge?*

Utterson spends much of the novel gathering evidence, in an informal fashion, about the Jekyll-Hyde relationship. All the evidence he collects points to the idea that Hyde is blackmailing Jekyll, which would explain why Jekyll turns pale whenever Hyde is mentioned. It would also explain why Hyde uses a personal check from Jekyll to pay off the parents of the girl he tramples and why Jekyll seems to be protecting Hyde after the Carew murder. Most important, it would explain why Jekyll has made a will that leaves his money to Hyde in the event of his death or "disappearance." Indeed, the will's reference to disappearance leads Utterson to assume that Hyde plans to murder Jekyll; there seems little else that could cause a respectable doctor simply to vanish. All of Utterson's deductions fit the facts at hand. They construe the Hyde-Jekyll connection as nothing more than the grip of a common criminal on his victim. They serve to make sense of a baffling situation, and they are reasonable.

But, of course, the reasonable nature of Utterson's deductions proves precisely their downfall. Utterson remains so adamantly rational and sensible that he never once admits the possibility of a supernatural explanation. He is the embodiment of the Victorian mind, which is either unable or unwilling to acknowledge the existence of the perverse or transgressive.

2. *Paying particular attention to Stevenson's descriptions of the city at night, discuss how Stevenson uses descriptive passages to evoke a mood of dread.*

At various junctures in *Dr. Jekyll and Mr. Hyde,* Stevenson uses vivid descriptions to evoke a sense of the uncanny and the supernatural, and of looming disaster. He first employs this technique in the opening scene, when Enfield relates his story of witnessing Hyde trample a little girl—a night when the streets were so empty that he began "to long for the sight of a policeman."

This notion of the city as a fearful landscape recurs throughout the novel. After hearing the tale of Mr. Hyde, Utterson suffers from dreams in which Hyde stalks through "labyrinths of lamplighted city," crushing children and whispering evil into Jekyll's ears. In Utterson's vision, London becomes a nightmare city, a place of terror where Hyde can perpetrate his crimes unchecked. The nightmare city reappears in Utterson's later, waking description of London. Leading the police to Hyde's apartment through a foggy predawn, Utterson watches the mist swirl and transform the neighborhood into "a district of some city in a nightmare," bringing a "touch" of "terror" even to the stolid policemen.

By the novel's final scene, these cityscapes connote not only terror but also foreboding of even more horrifying dangers. When Poole fetches Utterson to Jekyll's house, the wildness of the night and the empty streets fill the lawyer with "a crushing anticipation of calamity." In all these descriptions, Stevenson creates a perceptual dread that reinforces the conceptual horror of his subject matter.

3. *Discuss the narrative approach in the novel. What characterizes the way that events are reported? How does this method of narrative contribute to the thematic development of the novel?*

Much of *Dr. Jekyll and Mr. Hyde* is written in a brisk, businesslike, and factual way. Dry and forthright, the text often resembles a police report more than a novel. This colorlessness derives in part from the personality of Mr. Utterson, through whose eyes most of the story is told. Proper and upright, Utterson approaches the events with a desire to preserve any possible trace of orderliness or rationality in them. But the narrative's dry manner also seems to arise from the text itself. The original title of the novel, *The Strange Case of Dr. Jekyll and Mr. Hyde,* as well as chapter headings—including "Incident of the Letter" and "Incident at the Window"—seem to reveal an attitude of scientific detachment within the very structure of the novel. When the text presents the letters of Lanyon and Jekyll almost as if they were pieces of evidence, the story itself seems to become something of a scientific proof.

The attitude of formality and propriety in the narrative contrasts sharply with its mystical and uncanny content. With its prim demeanor, the text could be seen as attempting to repress or deny the subject matter that lurks inside it. Stevenson implies that a similar dynamic is at work in the Victorian Britain that he inhabits and portrays. The phenomenon plays itself out on the individual scale as well, of course—the existence of Hyde in the novel testifies to the existence of an evil or primitive aspect within each one of us, just barely hidden beneath a polite, unruffled exterior.

Quiz

1. What is Utterson's profession?
   A. Lawyer
   B. Doctor
   C. Priest
   D. Detective

2. With whom does Utterson take a weekly walk?
   A. Jekyll
   B. Lanyon
   C. Enfield
   D. Poole

3. What did Enfield see Hyde do late one night?
   A. Break into Jekyll's house
   B. Trample a girl
   C. Shoot a man
   D. Steal bread

4. Whom does Jekyll's will initially specify as his heir?
   A. Poole
   B. Lanyon
   C. Enfield
   D. Hyde

5. Why has Lanyon and Jekyll's friendship cooled?
   A. They had a dispute over Jekyll's scientific inquiries
   B. They both fell in love with the same woman
   C. Lanyon found Jekyll's run-down laboratory unsettling
   D. Jekyll stole Lanyon's research

6. How does Utterson first meet Hyde?
   A. He goes to Hyde's home
   B. They meet at a dinner party
   C. Utterson stakes out the door to Jekyll's laboratory, where Hyde has been known to come
   D. Hyde comes to Utterson with a legal question

7. How do the characters in the novel describe Hyde?
   A. They cannot describe him; they are struck by lightning when they utter his name
   B. They say he is ugly and deformed but cannot say exactly why
   C. They say he looks oddly similar to Jekyll—like a warped version of him
   D. They say he has an ugly scar across his face

8. When Utterson tells Jekyll that he has "been learning something of young Hyde," how does Jekyll respond?
   A. He laughs and says that Utterson is lying
   B. He claims never to have met Hyde
   C. He admits everything
   D. He turns pale and begs Utterson to change the subject

9. What does a servant girl witness from a window?
   A. Hyde murdering Sir Danvers Carew
   B. Jekyll and Hyde meeting in secret
   C. Jekyll transforming into Hyde
   D. Hyde trampling a little child

10. Who leads the police to Hyde's home?
    A. Jekyll
    B. A servant girl
    C. Utterson
    D. Enfield

11. What is Poole's position?
    A. He is Jekyll's lab assistant
    B. He is Jekyll's butler
    C. He is Utterson's clerk
    D. He is a detective

12. What happens to Hyde after the Carew murder?
    A. His body is found in the river
    B. He flees the country
    C. He kills Jekyll
    D. He disappears

13. What happens to Jekyll after the Carew murder?
    A. He becomes more sociable and devotes himself to good works
    B. He enters into a friendship with Enfield
    C. He abandons science
    D. He flees the country

14. What does Mr. Guest tell Utterson about the handwriting on the letter from Hyde?
    A. It has been forged
    B. It is a woman's handwriting
    C. It belongs to Jekyll
    D. It belongs to a left-handed person

15. What does Lanyon give Utterson before he dies?
    A. A box, not to be opened until Lanyon's death
    B. A letter, not to be opened until Jekyll's death or disappearance
    C. A small fortune
    D. A mysterious vial

16. In the weeks following his dinner party, what happens to Jekyll?
    A. He slowly poisons himself
    B. He begins plotting to kill Utterson
    C. He flees the country
    D. He locks himself in his laboratory and refuses to see anyone

17. Where do Enfield and Utterson see Jekyll one day during his seclusion?
    A. At Lanyon's funeral
    B. At the window of his laboratory
    C. In Hyde's apartment
    D. On a foggy street

18. Who summons Utterson to Jekyll's house near the end of the novel?
    A. Enfield
    B. Jekyll himself
    C. Poole
    D. Hyde

19. Why do the servants think that the man in the laboratory is not Jekyll?
    A. His voice is different from Jekyll's
    B. Jekyll is out of the country
    C. Jekyll is dead
    D. Jekyll never goes in the laboratory

20. Who does Utterson find in the laboratory after breaking down the door?
    A. Enfield
    B. No one
    C. Jekyll, lying dead
    D. Hyde, lying dead

21. What horrifying event does Lanyon write about having witnessed?
    A. The death of Danvers Carew
    B. Jekyll transforming into Hyde
    C. Hyde transforming into Jekyll
    D. Utterson killing himself

22. Who is Hyde?
    A. Jekyll's insane brother, whom he has tried to keep locked in the attic
    B. Jekyll's son born out of wedlock
    C. Jekyll's dark side, embodied in a separate being
    D. Jekyll in disguise

23. What brings Hyde into being?
    A. A potion, concocted by Jekyll
    B. A magic book
    C. A genie
    D. Incantations

24. Initially, why does Jekyll turn himself into Hyde?
    A. Poole forces him to do so
    B. He wants to escape his nagging wife
    C. He wants to kill Carew and Utterson
    D. He enjoys doing so

25. How does Jekyll deal with Hyde in the end?
    A. He has a priest exorcize Hyde
    B. He shoots Hyde
    C. He realizes the folly of becoming Hyde and decides to live the rest of his life as Jekyll
    D. Involuntarily, he becomes Hyde permanently, and then Hyde kills himself.

ANSWER KEY:
1: A; 2: C; 3: B; 4: D; 5: A; 6: C; 7: B; 8: D; 9: A; 10: C; 11: B; 12: D; 13: A; 14: C; 15: B; 16: D; 17: B; 18: C; 19: A; 20: D; 21: C; 22: C; 23: A; 24: D; 25: D

Suggestions for Further Reading

HAMMOND, J. R. *A Robert Louis Stevenson Companion: A Guide to the Novels, Essays, and Short Stories.* London: Macmillan, 1984.

HUBBARD, TOM. *Seeking Mr. Hyde: Studies in Robert Louis Stevenson, Symbolism, Myth, and the Pre-Modern.* Frankfurt: Peter Lang, 1995.

MAIXNER, PAUL, ED. *Robert Louis Stevenson, the Critical Heritage.* Boston: Routledge & Kegan Paul, 1981.

NABOKOV, VLADIMIR. *Lectures on Literature.* New York: Harcourt Brace Jovanovich, 1980.

NOBLE, ANDREW, ED. *Robert Louis Stevenson.* Totowa, New Jersey: Barnes and Noble, 1983.

SAPOSNIK, IRVING S. *Robert Louis Stevenson.* New York: Twayne Publishers, 1974.

VEEDER, WILLIAM R., AND GORDON HIRSCH. *Dr. Jekyll and Mr. Hyde: After One Hundred Years.* Chicago: University of Chicago Press, 1988.